The Value Growers

The Value Growers

Growers

Achieving Competitive Advantage Through Long-Term Growth and Profits

JAMES McGRATH

FRITZ KROEGER

MICHAEL TRAEM

JOERG ROCKENHAEUSER

McGraw-Hill

NEW YORK   SAN FRANCISCO   WASHINGTON, D.C.   AUCKLAND   BOGOTÁ
CARACAS   LISBON   LONDON   MADRID   MEXICO CITY   MILAN
MONTREAL   NEW DELHI   SAN JUAN   SINGAPORE
SYDNEY   TOKYO   TORONTO

Library of Congress Cataloging-in-Publication Data

The value growers : achieving competitive advantage through long-term growth and profits / James McGrath . . . [et al.].
   p.   cm.
   Includes index.
   ISBN 0-07-136440-4 (cloth)
     1. Corporations—Valuation.   2. Industrial management.   3. Corporate profits.
   4. Corporations—Growth.   5. Corporations—Growth—Case studies.   I. McGrath,
James, 1947–

   HG4028.V3 V35 2000
   658.15'5—dc21   00-060574

McGraw-Hill

A Division of The McGraw·Hill Companies

1 2 3 4 5 6 7 8 9 0 DOC/DOC 0 9 8 7 6 5 4 3 2 1 0

ISBN 0-07-136440-4

Printed and bound by R. R. Donnelley & Sons Company.

McGraw-Hill books are available at special quantity discounts to use as premiums and sales promotions, or for use in corporate training programs. For more information, please write to the Director of Special Sales, Professional Publishing, McGraw-Hill, Two Penn Plaza, New York, NY 10121-2298. Or contact your local bookstore.

This publication is designed to provide accurate and authoritative information in regard to the subject matter covered. It is sold with the understanding that neither the author nor the publisher is engaged in rendering legal, accounting, or other professional service. If legal advice or other expert assistance is required, the services of a competent professional person should be sought.
—*From a Declaration of Principles jointly adopted by a Committee of the American Bar Association and a Committee of Publishers.*

 This book is printed on recycled, acid-free paper containing a minimum of 50% recycled, de-inked fiber.

Contents

PART 3: THE FUTURE OF GROWTH

Foreword

When the authors of this book argue that growth is a basic fact of sound company life and that in a healthy company there is no way around it, I have to wholeheartedly agree from my experience. Kroeger, McGrath, Traem and Rockenhaeuser have reinforced what successful company leaders have felt for years. Growth is what finally establishes the value of a company, and growth is what every development should be based on.

Of course, there are other perspectives, and there have been times when these became very strong in companies around the world. Those were the times of cost-cutting and controlling, and no one should stand up and claim that cost-cutting and controlling are not important and are not important interferences with day-to-day processes and procedures. Of course, they are.

But what is more important and what decides the long-term well-being of a company is the strong internal impetus to grow. To follow a clear and compelling vision, follow an outreaching strategy, gain and retain customers, offer more and better products, provide outstanding service and invest in more—no, not of the same—but even better products and services and always expand in new markets—these are the growth drivers laid out in this book.

This natural impetus seemed to have been forgotten for a while, when many companies tried to counter fierce competition by putting even more pressure on their internal cost structures and the cost structures of their suppliers.

When in early 2000 I was a panelist at the World Economic Forum in Davos, Switzerland, I first heard about this book and the study underlying it. I immediately thought and still think this book has excelled in demonstrating how companies can regain their growth positions and thus improve their shareholder value, because it describes neither "empty," simple growth nor "pure" profit increase. Value building growth is what every company, traditional or dot.com, will have to pursue in these coming years. Economic development seems to set a healthy base for those who are willing to take the chance.

William W. George
Chairman and Chief Executive Officer
Medtronic, Inc.

Acknowledgments

After years of bottom-line orientation, it is high time for companies to reconsider top-line growth as an option. And whenever shareholder value assumes a high priority, it is time to think of value-building growth.

When this shift in the business climate began to evolve, we conducted a study managed by Dr. Joerg Rockenhaeuser, a principal in our Düsseldorf office, who was supported by Dr. Stefan Zeisel, Ross Waetzman, and Matthias Schubert. The results of the study were intriguing, so it did not take us long to decide to write a book. The team of authors was supported first and foremost by Dr. Marianne Denk-Helmold and Frank Luby, who shaped and finalized the manuscript with the help of Dirk Pfannenschmidt, Dr. Julia Kormann, Adriane Bergl, and Robin Black.

We are indebted to all our colleagues at A.T. Kearney.

Special thanks go to all practice and industry group leaders in our firm who contributed to the development of the cases that were documented by Frank Luby.

Once the manuscript was finished, Martha Peak from A.T. Kearney and Mary Glenn from McGraw-Hill guided it to publication.

Many thanks to everyone!

The authors

PART 1

The Growth Code

Navigating toward sustainable growth

YOUR GROWTH POTENTIAL IS VAST

If you want to open a serious discussion about your company's growth, you have very little to work with. There is simply not enough content. In contrast to the depth and richness of the discussion you could have on profit, a discussion on growth would probably yield very little. This is no surprise. Earnings have become such an obsession over the last decade that forecasting what businesses will earn has become an industry unto itself.

Many companies freely admit they have forgotten to grow the top line. Instead, they have undertaken a single-minded hunt for profitability based on cost reductions. Since September 1999 the management consulting firm A.T. Kearney has discussed corporate growth with over 350 CEOs and top managers at high-level meetings throughout Europe, Asia, and North America. This select group of corporate leaders estimates that they exploit no more than 50 percent of their company's growth potential. In other words, these managers—in the presence of their competitors and colleagues—said that their

3

companies should be growing twice as fast as they currently do! Why don't they pursue these opportunities? These companies point the finger at themselves. Instead of blaming outside forces, they cite their own strategies as the greatest barrier to growth and their own corporate structure as the most critical bottleneck.

Growth is an ever-changing enigmatic code that few managers have succeeded in cracking. Unlike profit, growth has no agreed-upon system of accounting. The profit-and-loss statement breaks down a revenue figure into earnings. No statement explains what went into building up that revenue figure, the so-called top line. How do we grow? And if we grow, how do we know it is the right kind of growth? There is no measure to account for it, no system to explain it, and no scientific approach to it.

In this context, modern financial theorists have come to the conclusion—following a mathematical model—that corporate revenue growth is a "random walk," unpredictable and beyond any manager's control. Large companies, say others, "hit a wall" when they reach a certain size. For no apparent reason, the magic evaporates, and they cease to grow. No sensible discussion about revenue growth will be possible until all definitions and causes and effects are sorted out. Without that discussion, growth will remain the random result of an alluring yet risky leap into the unknown.

Instead of venturing into this unknown to unlock their hidden growth potential, many companies have stuck to the tried-and-true compass settings. Instead of addressing growth and making it a priority to grow the top line, they choose to cut, slash, squeeze, and restructure their way to a higher bottom line. Ever since the concept of delivering shareholder value reached the forefront of management thinking, the understanding of both accounting and economic profit has exploded into a science. Misinterpreting Alfred Rappaport, companies adopted a multitude of choices for metrics—such as economic earnings or CFROI—to measure and manage their bottom line. To select and calculate such numbers, CEOs and their teams dip into the ever-expanding toolbox of techniques. They have also realized that managing internal and external expectations is critical to the creation of shareholder value. They employ investor relations managers and communications specialists. They have learned that surprises on the profit front—whether good or bad—indicate that management lacks a clear picture of the company's bearings. This usually has a strong impact on the share price.

But no one has ever explored what would happen to share price development if profit and growth were combined, rather than viewed as separate objectives. Corporate leaders know they could do better because they admit that their companies are missing out on the second half of their growth potential. Their frustrating challenge lies in making changes to crack the code and gain access to that hidden potential. Some CEOs have now begun to set profitable growth as their goal. The phrase is incorporated directly into the vision of companies such as the world's largest aluminum processor, Alcoa. But are companies really in a position to pursue profitability and growth as co-objectives?

Yes, they are. The key word is *balance.* When companies find the right balance between profit and growth as strategic co-objectives, they achieve what we refer to as *value-building growth.* By outperforming their peers in terms of growth while keeping an eye on the bottom line, the "value builders" create the greatest sustainable shareholder value over the long term. And that is what counts, both in today's and tomorrow's world.

Companies like Alcoa, Citigroup, and Nokia have made great strides in cracking the growth code. Our motivation for writing this book was to share what we have learned from such companies and to enable our readers to crack the growth code completely, in order to help them chart their own course for value-building growth.

We can provide new navigation tools and the right compass settings, developed from seeing how companies have successfully reset their own compasses to set sail in the right direction. Under full sail, they have become faster, nimbler, and harder to knock off balance as they explore their vast expanse of growth opportunities. These ships have safely reached new destinations—no matter what kind of climate they have had to weather.

Like *Hyperion,* the super yacht commissioned by Internet pioneer Jim Clark, value builders are dedicated to reshaping and redefining the way business is conducted. The team that designed and built *Hyperion* at the Netherlands' Royal Huisman Shipyard did not want to make a slightly better yacht with incremental improvements compared to others. They worked blank page to "look for new routes to further the art of sailing" and created a ship that combines speed, power, and luxury—supported by one of the largest computer networks ever assembled for nonindustrial use.

What did the team do after *Hyperion* had attracted worldwide attention? Naturally, they set out to push the limits even further. In November 1999, Clark commissioned the design and construction of *Athena,* a three-masted schooner set to outshine even *Hyperion.* The yachting team knows—like the value builders we have encountered—that the competition to gain and extend advantage has become not only more rewarding and much more intense but also never ending.

OVERCOMING GROWTH LIMITS: IT'S A QUESTION OF ATTITUDE

The knowledge about how to grow—and the appetite for it—was progressively lost as companies wound their way through the cost reduction and downsizing era of the 1970s and 1980s. This period stands out as an anomaly in the industrial era. Prior to the 1970s, industrial growth was accepted as a given. It raised living standards and would continue forever. A theoretical reflection on the nature and mechanics of industrial growth—which generations had taken for granted—did not begin in earnest until after the reconstructions that followed two world wars.

Many factors and influences combined to diminish growth's stature. Credit for one of them goes to the Club of Rome, a semipolitical think tank that conjured up Malthusian scenarios in the early 1970s about how environmental destruction and mass poverty would be inevitable if governments and industry leaders allowed economic growth to continue unabated. They called for the world to "promote harmony with nature" and concluded that "deliberately limiting growth would be difficult, but not impossible."

Viewed in the context of the early 1970s, a few of the Club of Rome's forecasts may have rung true. But the context has since changed beyond recognition. The Club of Rome had no inkling about the Internet, cellular communications, the mapping of the human genome, and space travel in reusable vehicles, even though the technologies for these breakthroughs had already begun to emerge. Instead, their sentiment at that time echoed the comment of the commissioner of the U.S. Patent Office at the end of the nineteenth century, who suggested that his office should be shut down because everything useful had already been invented. As the British economist Thomas Malthus had done some 150 years earlier, the Club of Rome likewise completely ignored human beings' innate ability to find their way around perceived barriers. By breaking them, dissolving them, ignoring them, or running headlong through them, people have always profited by eliminating barriers.

Nonetheless, the club's scary shadow reached into corporate boardrooms just long enough to effect an unfortunate change in mindset. Managers demoted growth to second-class status. To the extent that it remained desired at all, growth became a secondary goal for many companies. Cost and conservation rose to prominence, turning the 1970s into the frugal decade. Zero-based budgeting and overhead value analysis resulted in shrinkage that made some companies healthy and many others anorexic. Even well into the 1990s, frugality remained popular. Companies still had savings on their minds, and corporate diet pills such as business process reengineering

7

prevented revenue growth from gaining the top spot on the CEO's priority list.

As companies continue to swallow these diet pills, markets continue to swallow their message that the paragon of corporate excellence is leanness. The results of these reduction projects—and even the mere announcement that they have been planned—earn praise from equity investors and usually lead to a short-term boost in share prices. These interim blips are interpreted as the creation of actual shareholder value, but over the longer term this "value" proves to be ephemeral. In his thinking on shareholder value in the mid-1980s, Rappaport argued that companies cannot move forward by relying solely on the repeated optimization of their cost position. For whatever reasons, many companies chose to ignore Rappaport, favoring instead the "savings" mindset. These companies have converted only slowly to the idea that there is more to successful business than cost cutting.

It may sound obvious, but the alternative is for a company to grow, to put on muscle instead of fat. The true paragon of corporate excellence is strong and lean, not just lean. Neither strong nor lean is sufficient on its own to draw the very best from a company's resources and opportunities. Only those companies that balance strong and lean— and that realize that strong and lean are not mutually exclusive— outperform their peers and begin to navigate toward value-building growth.

The way companies develop, pursue, and exploit their growth opportunities provides a useful perspective from which to grasp the basics of value-building growth. Companies under the spell of cost orientation feel they communicate a sense of stability when they actually communicate complacency and resignation, which recalls the old cliché, "If it ain't broke, don't fix it." They become trapped or lulled into believing, similar to the Club of Rome, that their situation is static, so they should remain static as well. Stability reigns supreme.

To say that they seek a safe haven or a sure port is an apt analogy because the word *opportunity* is derived from the Latin expression "toward the port." Regardless of any regional differences or specific circumstances within their industry, how companies chart their courses in steering toward the ports has much in common with merchant sea captains.

- *Profit seekers.* These profit-oriented captains shuttle between safe, known ports and earn their money by optimizing their payloads and exerting tight control over their expenditures on crew and equipment. They sometimes behave as if they have no need to change their compass settings. They see no new ports to sail toward, no frontiers to conquer, and no new worlds to discover, explore, and map. They keep trying to make the same thing better.

- *Simple growers.* Some captains, in contrast, see new ports everywhere they look. They pay less attention to the size and makeup of the load or to the state of their crew than to simply keeping the fleet of ships sailing to as many harbors as possible. "More" is the watchword, not "better."

- *Underperformers.* Then, of course, many captains make it to the port either too late, with too little on board, or with second-rate crews. They may turn a small profit, but they never have the best places to dock, the best access to shipping lanes, or the highest-quality connections in the right places. Neither more nor better works consistently.

- *Value builders.* A fourth group of captains, however, decides to strike an uncompromising balance on all fronts. They secure the right payloads from the best customers, manage their crews, and constantly adjust their mix of old, established ports and new ports with high potential. They combine more with better.

Who has the best position among the four captains above? Is the balanced solution—which is analogous to *profitable growth* in current business terminology—truly better than the two extreme solutions, which focus either on maximizing top-line growth (simple growers) or on maximizing earnings (profit seekers)? We discovered that the balanced solution is indeed superior. The best companies have learned to balance more and better. They have learned to be strong and lean. A.T. Kearney's global Growth Study—detailed in Chapter 2—underscores the point that the extremes create less shareholder value in the long term. Neither an orientation toward pure profit growth nor toward growth at all costs represents the proper compass setting:

- *Pure profit growth.* Those who preach "maximize profit at all means" will have a hard time arguing their case before an astute board of directors, not to mention the smaller shareholders who will howl in protest at the annual general meeting. Today it is crystal clear: The mere optimization of cost blocks induced by a controller-driven mindset impedes growth steps in the short term. If allowed to take root over a longer period, it creates a climate that discourages risk taking and inhibits growth.

- *Growth at all costs.* Most companies that grow for growth's sake encounter severe difficulties. There are countless examples of unhealthy and unsustainable growth, which is sheer growth without regard for profitability. Companies such as Nintendo have discovered that efforts to get bigger and bigger in the growing consumer electronics industry will not result in sustained shareholder value creation if profitability does not follow.

The German retail group Karstadt—whose growth efforts via acquisitions led neither to superior growth nor to superior shareholder value creation—contrasts sharply with the French retailers such as Pinault-Printemps, Promodès, and Carrefour. These companies demonstrated impressively how shareholder value is created by generating top-line growth as well as growth in economic profit. To give themselves a greater operating scale and to create more opportunities,

Carrefour and Promodès merged in 1999. Their challenges will be discussed in greater detail in Chapter 6.

RESETTING YOUR COMPASS
TO VALUE-BUILDING GROWTH

All business leaders who have tried to tap their full growth potential know that determination is not enough. Growth-oriented thinking alone will not move a shareholder value curve even one tick upward. A company needs to change its mindset and find its balance before it can tap its hidden potential and achieve value-building growth.

Anyone who paid attention in Business 101 can rattle off approaches that should lead to growth: new products in old markets, old products in new markets, new products in new markets, new services for old products, old services for new products, and so on. Everyone is now aware of powerful marketing tools based on better and broader information technology. The umbrella concept e-business covers techniques such as data warehousing, data mining, micromarketing, and distribution of products and services through entirely new channels.

In this new context, every company should have a surplus of plain vanilla growth opportunities to choose from. But who wants only vanilla? In the great expanse beyond these opportunities lie other unique opportunities built on risk and innovation and sustained by the resulting competitive advantage. As business contexts change, mindsets need to change with them. In the emerging e-business world, advantage reigns supreme, not stability. The compelling risks and rewards of e-business add a special urgency for a company to stay and increase—not protect—its lead over its competitors.

The first step toward a new mindset is to embrace this great expanse of opportunity. Companies seeking to extend their advantages build their business models—their sailing ships—specifically to explore this expanse. Today's business leaders need to create an

11

entrepreneurial climate free from purely profit-oriented thinking. Tomorrow's leaders will need to exploit this climate to its limits. This new compass setting has to be combined with openness for opportunities, a high acceptance for new but unproven methods, and a very high tolerance of mistakes, the inevitable byproduct of successful exploration.

Value-building growth is definitely about balance. All other approaches to combining strong and lean fall short of maximizing the creation of shareholder value. If strong and lean cannot work together, a company cannot move forward.

The emergence of e-business makes value-building growth even more promising. What most companies see as a plus for their individual success is rapidly developing into a *sine qua non*. E-business turns competitive advantage into an endangered species by making the old advantages earned in old channels vanish overnight. For some, however, e-business will serve as a growth engine, just as telegraph and rail did a century ago. These nascent industries experienced double-digit growth over decades and became the building blocks of other new industries.

Those who seek a safe haven amid the e-business maelstrom will have found yet another excuse not to grow, along with timeworn classics such as "the environment," "the competition," or "the global economic situation." Those who adopt a me-too approach to e-business will be caught off guard when the distance between them and their best-performing peers widens from a gap to a gulf. The business press is filled with reports on companies that claim to have used e-business to jazz up their traditional business with a fancy new channel, but at the same time they remain puzzled that their commitment to this new trend has not translated into immediate growth and increased shareholder value. Against this backdrop, one question expresses the entire challenge that CEOs face as they look into the vastness of today's opportunities: "How do I grow?" This book answers that question from all aspects:

- Chapter 2, "Cracking the Growth Code," introduces the concepts of center of gravity, balance, and growth drivers. These three concepts underlie value-building growth. Companies use center of gravity and balance to orient themselves and to find the right route between revenue growth and profit. Their arsenal of growth drivers allows them to navigate, adjust their compass settings, and continue their journey.

- Part 2, "The Routes to Value-Building Growth," takes its name from the various approaches companies can take to value-building growth. These four chapters provide strategy and show-case examples of how companies changed their center of gravity, redirected their balance, and achieved value-building growth. Examples include the chocolate maker Hershey's, which broke the profit trap, FedEx, which overcame simple growth, and Nokia, which escaped from underperformance.

- Part 3, "The Future of Growth," explores current and future challenges. Chapter 7, "The Shape of Today," offers insight into dot.com companies that face two alternatives: Grow up or fold

---

Captain's Log Day 1   **Growth issues**

Dutch sea captains recorded their maps, notes, and undertakings in a router. Over the course of the book we will provide a series of quick takes to help you put together a router for your exploration of value-building growth.

- **Growth pays.** Our growth study revealed that value-building growth – superior revenue growth and value growth above peer group average – generates the most shareholder value over the long term.

- **Growth potential is vast.** CEOs throughout the world admit they use about half of their company's full growth potential.

- **Companies themselves are the biggest barriers.** These same CEOs admit that the biggest barriers and bottlenecks lie within their own companies.

- **E-business is urgent.** It not only helps bring growth back to the forefront, it also demands action.

- **The growth code has been cracked.** Value builders reveal how to unlock their hidden growth potential.

up. They need to show their ability to grow profitably, as Cisco, Sun Microsystems, and most recently Yahoo! have done. Even the dot.com world has its share of simple growers such as Excite@home and profit seekers such as America Online, which took a record-setting step toward rekindling its top-line growth when it announced a $150 bn merger with media giant Time Warner in early 2000. Chapter 8, "The Shape of Tomorrow," will describe the near future when e-business is commonplace. E-business, after all, is simply traditional business in disguise. When everyone is aboard, the "e" will disappear. Business will then live and die on its ability to generate value for customers and investors. E-business will become *v-business*.

Cracking the growth code

THE COMMITMENT TO VALUE-BUILDING GROWTH

It would be irresponsible and highly suspect of us to compile your Captain's Log and send you off on the quest for value-building growth before we had done some exploring of our own. Two years ago A.T. Kearney launched its ongoing Growth Study, which currently analyzes the performance of 20,000 companies worldwide, representing 98 percent of world market capitalization. To allow clear patterns to emerge, this initiative traces the companies' performance as far back as 1988. The study is also based on over 100 company analyses, as well as personal interviews with CEOs, top executives, and industry experts in Europe, Asia, and North America. (For more facts about our research, please see Appendix 1.)

The initial findings of the Growth Study rely on a more precise definition of *value-building growth*: A company is a value builder when it outperforms its peers both in revenue growth and in the creation of shareholder value. But what is shareholder value, and why and how does it relate to value-building growth?

VALUE-BUILDING GROWTH: WHY ARE REVENUE AND SHAREHOLDER VALUE IMPORTANT?

First, consider shareholder value. Since shareholders collectively "own" the firm in which they hold shares, it is only natural that they want to maximize the economic value of their holding. Just as ship owners take pride in their vessel, whether they intend to sell it, sail it, or simply keep it afloat, they must invest considerable resources to maintain it.

So what drives the value of a company? As with ships, many aspects must be considered. Are revenues growing? Are costs being kept at bay? Does this combination result in profit? Does management have a promising business plan? Is it on track to meeting its goals? Based on these aspects, a wide range of opinions exists on how to value a company.

The Growth Study began with a simple premise on firm valuation: The value of the firm is what the market will pay for it. Although this is not revolutionary, it does define a benchmark for measuring a successful company. Shareholder value is measured by a company's stock price with some adjustments for dividends. We call this measure *adjusted market capitalization* (AMC), and use the growth of AMC to track value growth.

Returning to our original question, we can now rephrase it to ask: What drives value growth? Current earnings streams explain at most 20 percent of a company's value. The rest is attributable to expected growth of profits. The extent of these as-yet-unrealized profits depends, in turn, on expected revenue growth. In other words, expected profit growth is linked more closely to revenue growth than to any other measure. Even if a company is not profitable today, or tomorrow, share prices move largely on the expectation of future profits, which are driven by expectations of future revenues.

Expected profit growth could arise partly from cost cuts, but costs can be cut only so far. In early 2000, the Coca-Cola Company announced plans to improve its profitability with a restructuring that would reduce worldwide staff by 20 percent. While investors praised these necessary actions, consider what would happen if Coke tried this strategy every year. Year after year, fewer and fewer people would need to work harder to run the global giant with fewer and fewer resources. Like an overworked machine, the stress would eventually take its toll. Coke's ability to compete would erode, and its ability to grow would suffer. Needless to say, such situations seldom go over well with investors.

Unlike growth through cost cutting, however, the boundaries of revenue growth are virtually nonexistent. As long as good ideas are transformed into sales, profits can follow. But over the long term, companies need to invest in order to grow. This is highly evident in industries like biotechnology and among technology firms like America Online. AOL's merger with Time Warner has the primary aim of achieving future sales. At the time this book was being written, the U.S.-U.K. cellular operator Vodafone was keen on acquiring Germany's Mannesmann conglomerate in order to do the same. Mannesmann originally argued that it could achieve higher future profits—and create more value—by remaining independent instead of being absorbed into Vodafone. That conflict ended in February when Mannesmann's board approved a modified merger agreement with Vodafone, resulting in what was then the largest merger in history.

Managers and shareholders both care about maximizing the company's value. However, pursuing this goal through cost cutting alone is myopic; cost cutting alone can trim only so much weight from your ship before you lose vital components. A balance must instead be struck between growth and weight reduction, between strong and lean. By continuing to bring innovations to market, sound companies add the strength that creates value and results in value-building growth.

ACHIEVING VALUE-BUILDING GROWTH: WHO HAS DONE IT?

The four philosophies of the captains in the previous chapter strongly influence whether they consistently outperform their competitors. The same applies to companies. Imagine a map where the captain's philosophies represent four distinct regions, or compass points. How a company performs not only reflects its mindset but also determines the region to which the company belongs. If we look at where the companies sail based on their performance in terms of revenue growth and value creation, the map would look like the matrix in Figure 2-1.

The value builders achieve both above-average revenue growth and above-average growth in shareholder value over long periods. The perfectly average company sits at the crosshairs of the matrix. It has revenue growth exactly equal to the revenue average, and it also enjoys value growth equal to the average of its industry peers. The value builders constantly try to extend their advantages and push them-

Growth matrix (CAGR 1988–1998)

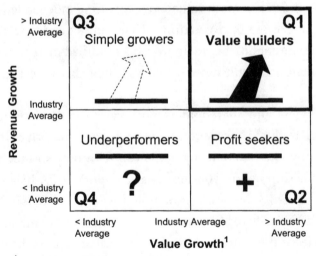

[1] Measured as Adjusted Market Capitalization Growth = market capitalization growth adjusted for change in equity.

Figure 2-1 The A.T. Kearney Growth Matrix.

selves farther into the upper right, trying to put as much distance as possible between themselves and the center. They do this by consistently finding ways to stay ahead of their peers in the competition for growth opportunities, capital, and talent.

The profit seekers rely on established ports and have perfected the art of keeping tight control over their crew. They show revenue growth rates below their industry average, although they still create significant shareholder value. The simple growers send out a reconnaissance team to plant a flag every time they sight land. They manage to outperform their peers in generating revenue, but over time the once anticipated profit fails to follow. Thus, the companies rank below their industry's average for creating shareholder value. And what happens to the underperformers? Relatively speaking, they are below average on both counts: revenue growth and shareholder value creation since 1988. They move in exactly the opposite direction as the value builders.

Even some of the less successful captains manage to keep their ships—and their businesses—afloat by earning a slim profit or expanding their reach in absolute terms. These captains need to remember, however, that they are competing not just for growth opportunities but for the other scarce resources as well: capital, knowledge, skills, and leaders. Their absolute performance will still leave them at a disadvantage if their direct competitors consistently outperform them. The battle revolves not around the question "How much?" but rather around the question "How much more?"

What happens if we replace ships with companies, as we did with the world's largest retailers in the previous chapter? Figure 2-2 shows the position in the Growth Matrix for several internationally known companies, positioned against their respective industry averages. These matrices provide a bird's-eye view of a company's development over the 11-year period from 1988 onward. It comes as no surprise that a company such as Microsoft, which has grown to roughly US$ 500 bn in market capitalization and $18 bn in revenues, ranks as a value builder. In a sector in which many companies have experienced rapid revenue growth and spawned legions of paper millionaires, Microsoft still outperforms on a regular basis. The antitrust case before the U.S. Justice Department raises the question of how the so-called Baby Bills will perform if the remedy is indeed a break-up of the company. If previous breakups such as Standard Oil and AT&T provide any guidance, the Baby Bills will continue the value-building growth tradition established by Microsoft.

In contrast to Microsoft, the U.S. toy retailer Toys "R" Us has continued to grow, but it is having difficulty convincing investors that its business model—once considered a breakthrough—still works the way it once did. The company has been slow to change, and it is now under pressure from traditional competitors and e-tailers. In 1998, Toys "R" Us lost its market leadership in the United States to the general retailing giant Wal-Mart. During the 1999 holiday season, it received stiff competition from eToys and even from Amazon.com. Toys "R" Us also demonstrates how gains in absolute revenue performance do not necessarily lead to value-building growth. The

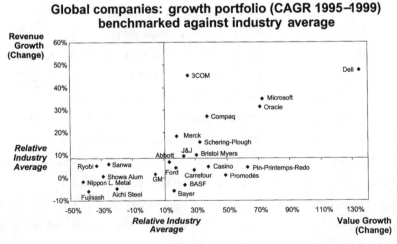

Figure 2-2 The position of selected, well-known companies in the Growth Matrix.

company's stores saw a strong upturn in sales in 1999 thanks to the Pokémon games and toys. But so did the competition. Hot trends and hot toys alone did not help the company regain its top position.

If you combine industries within countries or regions, clusters emerge in the matrix, as shown in Figure 2-3. These clusters mirror the economic developments in the particular region, again viewed from an 11-year perspective. The U.S.-based high-tech companies Dell, Oracle, and Microsoft have a combined market capitalization of over $600 bn, and they continue to produce double-digit revenue growth. Instead of hitting a wall, these companies have run right through barriers that have supposedly caused other companies' revenue growth to slow down or stop. All three of these high-tech pioneers are young enough to still be firmly run by their founders, whereas examples of wall hitters like Kodak and Kellogg (not shown in the figure) have been around for 100 years or more.

A cluster of German conglomerates straddles the profit seekers and the underperformers. Latecomers to the ongoing obsession with

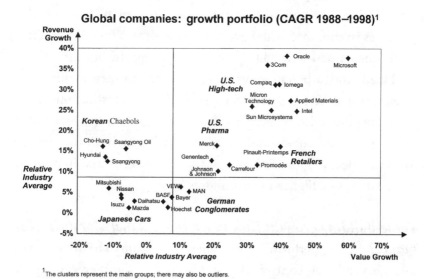

¹The clusters represent the main groups; there may also be outliers.

Figure 2-3 Where to find the value builders.

earnings, large German companies have tried to make up for lost time by keeping their sights on year-end results. After World War II, German companies unfurled their sails and regained world leadership in many industries by focusing on innovation and geographic expansion. They made "Made in Germany" synonymous with "high-quality products." Their focus then shifted dramatically toward stability instead of advantage. Growth for quite a while has been a secondary issue for them. While they have grown cautiously and conservatively, they have watched much of their advantage erode.

Some of the larger units of the Korean family-dominated *chaebol* conglomerates, meanwhile, will go down in history as benchmarks for the damage caused by simple growth. In their efforts to push revenues ever higher, the companies ran up astronomical debt-to-equity ratios, which left them vulnerable to a whole range of financial and economic shocks, from the Asian currency crisis over the plunge in prices for computer chips to the commoditization of plastic resins. Daewoo, at its zenith, left its mark on industries ranging from semiconductors to clothing to cars. This pursuit of unbridled growth has left the company so financially strapped that its creditors began in mid-1999 to trim the organization, business by business. The company had stretched its resources so thin that it had over $50 bn in debt. When the creditors are finished, Daewoo will likely produce nothing else but cars.

Finally, the turbulent waters of the underperformers include a few Japanese carmakers and several Japanese financial institutions. These companies did indeed generate some revenue growth and shareholder value. But they consistently lagged behind their European and American peers in those areas, and they did not succeed in resetting the compass to a higher value-building course.

Value-building growth: How much room is there for outperformance?
Underperforming companies often claim to be the victims of forces beyond their control. They put blame on almost everything: the macroeconomy, the Russian and Asian financial crises, and the unfore-

seen moves of competitors. Insurers, food processors, and utility companies even get to legitimately blame the weather from time to time for declines in their short-term performance.

So what do these companies do while pointing a finger at Alan Greenspan, Mother Nature, or someone else? They pinch and stretch their resources in the interest of saving and conserving. They pursue efficiency synergies, which in most cases involve cost cutting and repeated restructuring. After years they might find themselves managing a lean organization that is highly productive and resourceful and runs on a shoestring. In that case, the company has achieved its goal. The problem is, at some point, it has no place left to go.

This purely profit-oriented mindset ignores the existence of the hidden potential the CEOs in our discussions know is attainable. The A.T. Kearney Growth Study quantified this hidden half by showing just how much room companies in various industries have to improve their performance. In other words, companies have many options, if they would only look for them. Figure 2-4 shows where the untapped growth potential—the hidden half—lies for many companies that have set their bearings toward something other than value-building growth. Figure 2-5 shows what these companies have forsaken in terms of value creation.

Companies in so-called sluggish or smokestack industries often use such labels as an excuse for below-average growth, risk-averse behavior, and a sort of "sit-on-our-hands" mindset. You almost come to believe these companies are not supposed to grow. But value builders exist in very mature industries. To comprehend what this means in pure dollars, take the example of the paper industry, which has one of the narrowest growth ranges of all industries. Assume that two paper companies had the same market capitalization in 1988. Over the next decade, one company remained at the crosshairs of the Growth Matrix by seeing its shareholder value grow at exactly the industry average. Its chief competitor saw its value rise by 10 percent faster than the industry average, year on year. By 1998, the faster

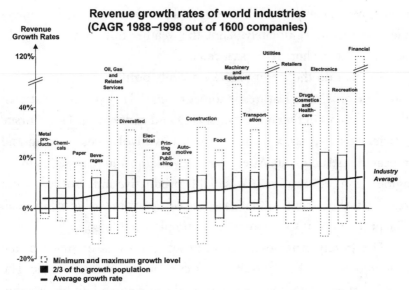

Figure 2-4   Every industry has potential for superior revenue growth.

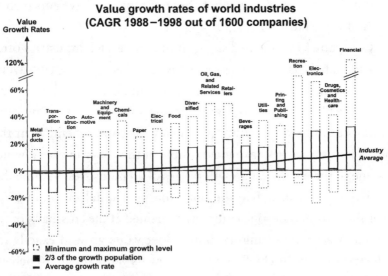

Figure 2-5   Every industry has potential for superior value growth.

grower would be worth around 2.5 times as much as its competitor. While one company grew into, say, a group with $10 bn, its faster-growing competitor would have reached a value of around $25 bn.

That difference of $15 bn is precisely the reason that companies need to move themselves away from the crosshairs in the matrix. They need to become value builders. The accelerated pace of the e-business world is extremely adept at turning million-dollar gaps into billion-dollar gulfs in no time. Failure to realize this point leads a company in one of two directions. Either the company falls into the profit trap by continuing to recycle itself instead of reinventing itself, or the company joins the underperformers.

This underscores our main motive for developing the concepts of center of gravity and balance, which will be introduced in this chapter and illustrated with case examples in Part 2. Value-building growth does not happen accidentally. It is the product of a conscious, constantly monitored process in which success breeds success and in which value builders make their own luck. Value builders ride out economic downturns and the effects of other external influences. Their balanced and conscious control over the process of value-building growth inoculates them against the effects of external developments by allowing them to respond more quickly and confidently. They turn these downturns or macroeconomic events into new opportunities.

Contrary to the headlines that companies like eBay generate, entry into a "hot" sector such as computer software, e-business, or biotechnology does not automatically mean that the company will reach the point where it launches a well-received initial public offering (IPO) that makes the founders multimillionaires overnight. Many of these companies have yet to make a sustainable profit. Figures 2-4 and 2-5 show that every industry also has plenty of room to host under-performers.

Value-building growth: What are the rewards? If growth opportunities are ubiquitous and any company can become a value builder, well, so what? The universality of value-building growth does not explain why a company should strive for it nor how it should go about the many tasks involved. In other words, what incentive does a CEO have to abandon a profit orientation or a broad plan of diversification in favor of one geared more toward focused revenue growth? Why bother? Why should growth be an overwhelming imperative instead of simply nice to have?

There are some hard numbers on exactly what role revenue growth plays in the creation of shareholder value. There are also some "soft" reasons that superior revenue growth makes a dramatic difference. First of all, strong, stable growth is the decisive driver behind share prices over the long term. An individual company's relative revenue growth and its relative growth in shareholder value—as defined on the basis of adjusted market capitalization—show a strong correlation that increases over time.

In more hands-on terms, the shareholder value of the value builders increased at an average annual rate of 22.2 percent, compared with 14.7 percent for the profit seekers (see Figure 2-6). One might find that the return of 14.7 percent for the profit seekers is acceptable, especially considering their below-average growth. In reality, this apparent comfort zone of the profit seekers is a dangerous illusion. The risk of falling back toward underperformance is especially acute when a company brings a wave of cost cutting to a close, or it completes a long and complicated merger integration, only to realize that it lacks new growth initiatives or new ways to turn. These companies have focused on the finite area of cost cutting for so long that they have neglected the virtually infinite area of growth opportunities.

Revenue growth, in other words, provides the strong element we described in Chapter 1. A value builder, however, does not ignore the lean element. In fact, value builders understand the interaction between strong and lean as strategic co-objectives. There are clear limits on how lean a company can become, and the law of diminishing returns sets in rather quickly. This explains why the pursuit of

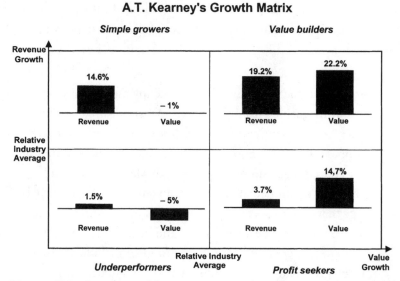

Figure 2-6 Strong, stable revenue growth triggers superior share price performance.

higher returns through constant efficiency seeking and cost cutting has a limited—albeit quantifiable—upside.

While lean is capped, the strong revenue growth has no such clear limits. The value builders such as Microsoft or Cisco have broken the law of diminishing returns over the last two decades. Their superior revenue growth has done more to boost their returns than any cost-cutting or efficiency program could ever have achieved. The acquisition philosophy of Cisco CEO John Chambers reflects this point. While merging companies in other industries make the synergy potential the centerpiece of the merger, Chambers focuses almost exclusively on the growth potential.

The finding that the long-term-growth trend is the main driver behind share prices creates a compelling reason for CEOs to shift the strategic balance of their company in favor of revenue growth. But CEOs should not pursue revenue growth simply because the mathematics work out best. There is also considerable qualitative evidence that investors prefer companies with a solid long-term-growth trend to companies whose balance is weighted much more heavily in favor of profit:

- *Growth is attractive.* Value builders occupy the first nine spots on *Fortune* magazine's list of "America's Most Admired Companies." Some 26 of the companies on *Fortune*'s list of the "100 Best Companies to Work For" are likewise value builders. While all four types of companies in the Growth Matrix offer their employees an immediate and difficult challenge, the one challenge that employees tend to prefer is value-building growth. Value builders exude a confidence and optimism that simply makes people want to come to work and contribute. It also makes a company an attractive partner for alliances or mergers. If managed properly, this image rubs off on customers as well.

- *Growth is invigorating.* Where there's growth, there's action, not reaction. By definition, a company that continually outperforms its peers—regardless of the industry—is a leader, not a follower. These companies operate at the cutting edge, where markets change and new processes and products are introduced. They push the envelope and actively seek out people and partners who want to help them push limits even further.

- *Growth means "upside" across the board.* Many companies have broken new ground in offering employees an attractive working environment. In many companies you can now bring your kids and even your dog to work, assuming you even "go" to work at all. But fun and lifestyle are not the only success factor in employee recruitment. The financial side will always matter. And companies who succeed in maintaining value-building growth naturally have more options and flexibility in terms of incentives such as bonuses, stock options, and stock purchase plans.

The extreme cases are the so-called dot.com stocks, where business models are radically different from traditional models and expectations for growth run high. Investors severely punish very profitable companies such as Dell Computer only when the future growth—not the profit trend—looks shaky. Traditional companies suffer this fate as well. The sudden and relatively steep decline of shares in Daimler-Chrysler in the summer of 1999 came partly because investors and analysts saw the company's medium-term pipeline—its well of growth opportunities—as relatively weak compared to its main competitors. In short, growth gives many companies a real competitive advantage in the market for tomorrow's scarce resources. They have an attractiveness, a visibility, and a flexibility that companies from the other regions of the Growth Matrix cannot match over the long term.

Captain's Log Day 2 — **Value-building growth**

Growth opportunities are not scarce. In fact, growth is possible under nearly all conditions, in any industry, in any region, and at any phase of a business cycle.

There is no excuse for not growing! Forget all of the jargon used to describe industries — sexy, smokestack, twilight, bricks and mortar, and hitting the wall. These blanket, long-accepted excuses for poor performance are now obsolete.

Strong, stable growth is the decisive factor behind share prices. This answers the CEO's question on whether to tip the scales in favor of revenue growth or a profit focus. The decisive factor behind the movement of share prices is a company's long-term growth trend, not the trend in its expected earnings.

YOUR CENTER OF GRAVITY REVEALS YOUR COMMITMENT TO GROWTH

The dots in the Growth Matrices such as Figures 2-2 and 2-3 are snapshots of companies. But they represent more than the compression of a company's history of growth and share price performance into one single point. They also mark the company's center of gravity—its orientation, its mindset, its reputation—over the period measured. In short, the company's commitment to growth and its success in executing that commitment are summed up in that single point. Through the choices they make and the strategies they undertake, companies essentially become the merchant sea captains who lend their names to the regions in the Growth Matrix. Ford, aggregated over the last 10 years, has been only a moderate value builder, while Exxon and General Motors were profit seekers. A widely acclaimed growth company such as the U.S. conglomerate General Electric has been a value builder, but barely.

The movements of the individual companies over time, however, are even more intriguing. Consider Microsoft, for example. For any given year, we determined Microsoft's revenue growth rate and value growth rate relative to its competitors. These numbers are shown in Table 2-1 for the first four years of the Growth Study.

If we then place these four dots in the matrix, they have the positions shown in Figure 2-7. By connecting the dots for the first three periods, we have a triangle. We form a similar triangle for the next three periods, and so on until the present. The midpoint of the middle of these triangles is Microsoft's center of gravity during the period for which the dots formed the triangle. For the time period 1988 to 1991, Microsoft's center of gravity rested at point *A*; it then shifted to point *B* for the period 1989 to 1992, as shown in Figure 2-8.

Looking at revenue and value growth over time, it becomes apparent that most companies migrate between the different areas, as Microsoft started to do in Figure 2-9. This migration means that although a company has been a value builder on average since 1988—

Table 2-1 Microsoft's Performance versus Its Competitors

Period	Revenue growth vs. industry average, %	Value growth vs. industry average, %
1988–1989	+27	+42
1989–1990	+26	+85
1990–1991	+47	+120
1991–1992	+40	−3

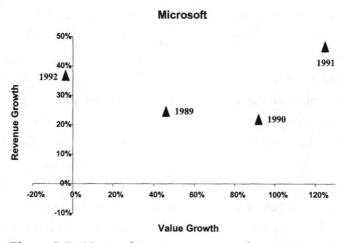

Figure 2-7 Microsoft's year-on-year performance.

the midpoint of an area defined by 10 dots—it probably spent some of its time positioned as a simple grower, a profit seeker, or an underperformer. Only a very small number of companies actually remained value builders—that is, kept their center of gravity in the upper right region of the matrix—for 10 or more consecutive periods. In other

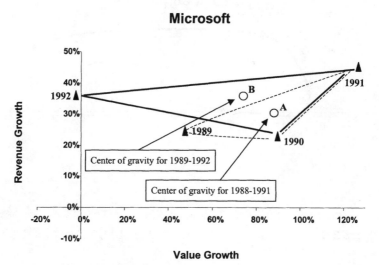

Figure 2-8 Changing centers of gravity.

words, it is extremely difficult for a company to consistently outperform its peers in revenue growth and shareholder value creation year after year.

Even Microsoft, the poster child of shareholder value creation, did not always outperform its industry peers. Table 2-1 shows that Microsoft's value growth was already 3 percent below the industry average from 1991 to 1992. More years of underperformance followed. As Figure 2-9 shows, Microsoft slightly underperformed its peer group in terms of value growth for the period 1991 to 1994 as a whole, shifting the company's center of gravity into the region of the simple growers. The dots on the curve in Figure 2-9 represent Microsoft's average performance over a three-year period. In other words, they indicate how robust the company's performance has been over the medium term.

Why did Microsoft fall out of favor with investors in this period? The decline reflects a series of events in this crucial period in the company's history. First, Microsoft launched its extensive investments

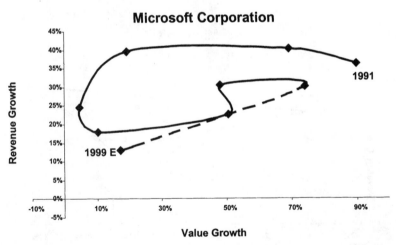

Figure 2-9   The migration of Microsoft since 1991 (average of three years).

in the development of *Windows 95* during this period. The emergence of *UNIX* had begun to erode Microsoft's dominant position in operating systems, while antitrust regulators blocked some of the company's expansion plans. Microsoft recovered strongly, however, as the curve in Figure 2-9 further shows. The company has come full circle, as its center of gravity for the three-year period ending in 1998—as shown by the dot in Figure 2-9—has been almost as strongly positioned as the company's center of gravity in 1991.

The movements of the center of gravity unravel another aspect of the growth code: Growth is not linear. It evolves in a spiral. At the top part of the spiral path, which the center of gravity traces, the value builders are truly sailing full speed ahead. They enjoy the double positive of vigorous growth and broad acceptance among investors. The consolidation periods occur when the center of gravity moves from the value-building growth region into profit seeking or into simple growth, as Microsoft's did. This happens when the company's growth slows or it falls temporarily out of favor with the markets.

In these situations, value builders such as Microsoft seize opportunities to realign their resources. They work to establish a better understanding of the market dynamics, then refine or redefine their strategies to make sure their temporary loss of favor or their temporary drag of growth does not become permanent. They prepare in this manner for spiraling up to the next wave of growth. The British services company Rentokil now faces a similar challenge. After a strong run of value-building growth, Rentokil's center of gravity has begun shifting rapidly toward simple growth, as shown in Figure 2-10. When sufficient data from 1999 become available to determine the next shift, Rentokil's center of gravity will have continued on its rapid course toward the lower left side of the matrix. Whether Rentokil manages to trace the kind of spiral Microsoft did depends entirely on whether the company can restore its balance, a theme we will discuss later in this chapter.

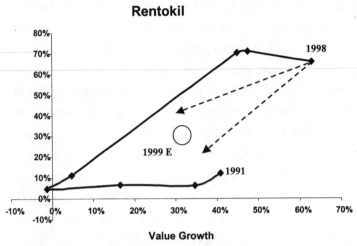

Figure 2-10 Rentokil's growth movements.

Rentokil

For more than 13 years, Rentokil embraced value-building growth in a way few other companies have. The goal of the company was loud and clear: "Increase sales and profits by 20 percent per year."

Rentokil, originally a services company focused on pest control and waste management, grew principally through acquisitions. In this manner the company expanded into over 40 countries and diversified into a wide range of services. One of the most spectacular acquisitions was the 1996 hostile takeover of British competitor BET, which created the world's largest supplier of business services. The purchase of BET was meant to ensure that the growth goal of 20 percent per year would be consistently met in subsequent years. Analysts, however, considered this move to be the wrong response to declining growth rates in Rentokil's original core business, pest control.

In the first half of the 1998 financial year, Rentokil missed the target of 20 percent growth for the first time in 12 years. Although the company barely fell short of the 20 percent mark, the markets pounded the stock and shaved off half of the company's market value within eight months. The plunge brought strategic weaknesses to light, which should have been recognized earlier. The heavy reliance on acquisitions to meet the growth targets left the company overdiversified. The company's rather military management style and its tying of employee compensation to a small number of performance measures diverted attention from the growth barriers the company faced: Its important markets were saturated, and it was running out of acquisition targets.

A restructuring and a strategic realignment could help the company return to a position of value-building growth. CEO Sir Clive Thompson, who earned the nickname "Mr. 20 Percent," said that in the future, the company will focus more on service quality and less on pure top-line growth.

It is rare indeed for a company to turn a spiral so tight that it maintains its position as a value builder over an entire 10-year period. Only Clear Channel Communications, a U.S.-based media company, succeeded in doing so, as Figure 2-11 shows. Many other highly prized companies over the last decade fell well short of that target. If we look at Clear Channel Communications' spiral, as in Figure 2-12, we see that it shows no signs of making the kind of "left turn" that Microsoft and Rentokil have done. In Chapter 6 we will describe in more detail how Clear Channel rose from the owner of one radio station in Texas to a multi-billion-dollar media empire.

The second most valuable corporation in the world, the U.S.-based conglomerate General Electric, also fell well short of the goal of achieving value-building growth year after year. In fact, it spent less than half of the 1990s as a value builder, as the spiral in Figure 2-13 shows.

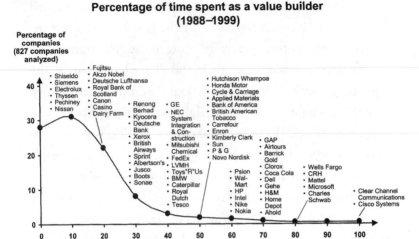

Figure 2-11 Value builders' staying power.

General Electric

The U.S. conglomerate General Electric was fending off the effects of a U.S. recession at the beginning of 1990. The measures that CEO Jack Welch undertook to reignite the company's growth hint that what CEOs around the world have told us is indeed true:

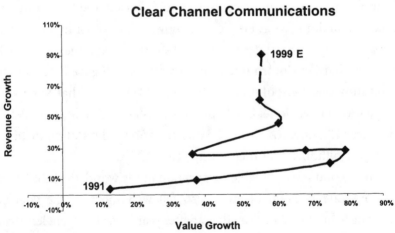

Figure 2-12 Clear Channel Communications continues to spiral up.

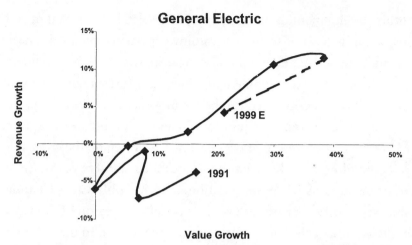

Figure 2-13 GE spent time as a profit seeker and underperformer before spiraling up.

The biggest barrier to growth is the company's own organization. Welch launched the "Work Out" restructuring initiative of streamlining the organization and empowering employees. As this move began to pay dividends, he raised the hurdle for performance: 15 percent operating margin, and 10 inventory turns.

Despite an economic slowdown in Europe a couple of years later, GE invested heavily in its expansion plans there, further stretching the company's resources. It also parted ways with its Kidder Peabody financial unit in 1994, bringing further focus to the organization. By 1995, investors had begun to buy into the idea that a company as large as GE could really transform itself into a growth company. And with the immense support of its GE capital unit, it did. The company's overall revenues grew from around $60 bn in 1994 to $112 bn in 1999. In 2000, investors made GE the world's most valuable company.

In 1999, two years before his retirement in April 2001, Jack Welch prescribed that all business processes in the Group be converted to the Internet, thus making another extremely important move for the future development of his company. Jack Welch believes that during his career he has not seen the economy experience such a dramatic change as at present due to the worldwide networking of computers. And, thanks to the development of e-business, the richest company of the world is well positioned for the coming change of leadership.

This finding raises a question: When value builders migrate, where do their centers of gravity go, and how often do they return to value-building growth? What shape does their spiral have over time, and how large is it? As we mentioned above, only Clear Channel survived the 1990s without ever having left the region of the value builders. If the company's center of gravity moves into the region of the simple growers, it stands a fair chance of returning. Out of the companies that moved away from value-building growth and returned, some 53 percent saw their spiral move much the same way Microsoft's did and Rentokil's has begun to.

In other words, these companies temporarily became simple growers, which indicates that these companies decided at least to not shut down their growth engines. This decision is intelligent and will pay off because it is hard to shift from a nongrowth orientation back to a stronger growth orientation. Those who actually decide to shut down their growth engine to pursue profit instead will need to maintain a profit-oriented focus, implementing all the measures that such an orientation entails: heavy cost cutting and aggressive belt tightening to meet earnings targets. The center of gravity thus reflects the company's commitment to growth.

History shows that pursuing profit rather than growth means cuts to R&D, a reining in of geographic expansion, and a hesitance to pursue riskier ventures. It means, in other words, that the company pulls the plug on all the elements that fueled value-building growth in the first place: It lowers its sails, assigns the crew odd jobs until it can dismiss some of them, and tries opportunistically to reach one nearby harbor. The change of mindset chokes off the entire spirit of action and growth. (See Figure 2-14.)

Out of the companies that moved away from value-building growth and returned, some 38 percent were underperformers, but only 9 percent were the obviously more complacent profit seekers. As William W. George, the chairman and CEO of Medtronic, described it, companies cannot switch on the growth initiatives like an electrical switch. Once they break their growth momentum, they have lost it for many years. A company should never break its growth culture or cut its investments in growth because growth is not something it can just kick start.

George's insight reflected other companies' experiences. One top manager described abandoning growth as "the biggest mistake we ever made in the history of our company": consciously slowing down or hindering their revenue growth. Thus, if growth means sacrificing the bottom line for a certain period, then do it. In the consolidation phases or fall-back periods, the true value builders never slow down their growth engine, even if it means sacrificing the bottom line over a certain

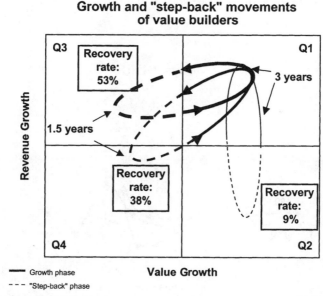

Figure 2-14 Which positions in the Growth Matrix are sustainable?

period. This is exactly what Microsoft did. Instead of stopping projects, it poured money into *Windows 95*. Instead of scaling back growth plans, Microsoft reached a point where others—in this case, the antitrust authorities—stepped in to stop them. Microsoft knows that falling into profit-seeking territory makes a return to value-building growth both slower and more difficult. Once the growth engine has been slowed down, it is often years before it is fired up again.

The spirals that the centers of gravity trace provide a useful way to compare the performance of two competitors at one glance. They bring to life the earlier example of how Toys "R" Us lost its market leadership to Wal-Mart, as shown in Figure 2-15. Wal-Mart regularly outgrew other large retailers throughout the 1990s, although the margin of outperformance narrowed in the mid-1990s. Toys "R" Us, in contrast, has barely kept pace with its competitors and has clearly fallen out of favor with investors. Toys "R" Us languishes in this area. Its center of gravity currently lies on the border between simple growth and underperformance, at a certain distance from the value-building growth position Wal-Mart still enjoys.

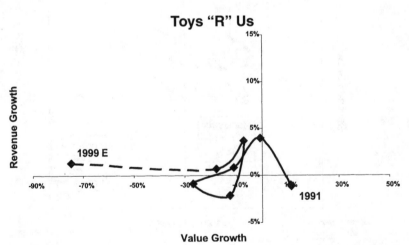

Figure 2-15 The centers of gravity for Toys "R" Us and Wal-Mart, 1991 to 1999.

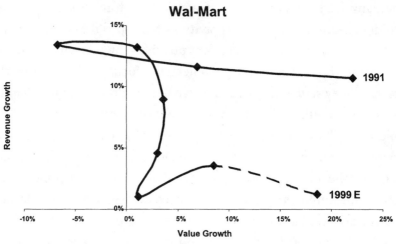

Figure 2-15 (*Continued*).

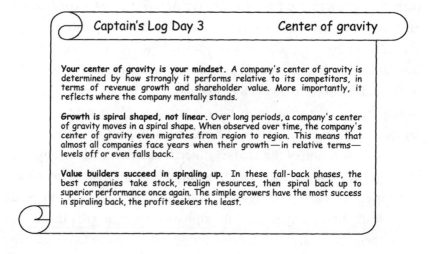

Captain's Log Day 3   Center of gravity

Your center of gravity is your mindset. A company's center of gravity is determined by how strongly it performs relative to its competitors, in terms of revenue growth and shareholder value. More importantly, it reflects where the company mentally stands.

Growth is spiral shaped, not linear. Over long periods, a company's center of gravity moves in a spiral shape. When observed over time, the company's center of gravity even migrates from region to region. This means that almost all companies face years when their growth—in relative terms—levels off or even falls back.

Value builders succeed in spiraling up. In these fall-back phases, the best companies take stock, realign resources, then spiral back up to superior performance once again. The simple growers have the most success in spiraling back, the profit seekers the least.

MAINTAINING YOUR BALANCE MEANS MANAGING YOUR COMMITMENT

The relationship sounds strikingly simple. If the spiral of a company's center of gravity shows a trend toward value-building growth, the company is balanced. If it is moving in any other direction, the company needs to adjust—immediately—to restore its balance. Value builders keep their center of gravity in the top right corner of the matrix—as far from the crosshairs as possible—by achieving a proper balance in three areas: strategic objectives, focus, and their growth arsenal. They strike their own balance between revenue growth and profitability with the understanding that these must be mutual co-objectives. They achieve a balanced focus by remembering that they are the masters of their own destiny. Outside factors might set the stage, but the internal factors ultimately determine the outcome of the show. Value builders also remain balanced across an array of internal growth drivers that form the basis for their growth determination, stakeholder empathy, and enabling business model—what we collectively refer to as the *growth arsenal.*

Revenue growth and profitability: Mixing strong and lean?

Striking a balance between revenue growth and earnings is a strategic challenge for every CEO. Some look enviously at highly valued dot.com companies that show triple-digit growth but make no money. Others take pride in their efforts to boost efficiency and keep the bottom line healthy to stay lean. If the score in this game is ultimately measured by the creation of shareholder value, who has the right approach?

The first section of this chapter noted that consistently strong and stable growth is the decisive factor behind the creation of shareholder value over the long term. Figure 2-14 in the previous section showed empirically that companies that emphasize revenue growth—even when their shares are underperforming—return more frequently to a position of value-building growth than other companies do. Those that choose to lower their sails in order to focus on efficiency and the bottom line fail to return to a position of value growth more than 90 percent of the cases.

But one should not jump to quick conclusions. The suggestion that a CEO merely needs to make a shift in strategic emphasis toward growth and away from a bottom-line orientation oversimplifies a much more complex issue. First of all, no CEO anywhere in the world walks in the door one morning, boldly adds the line "Folks, we're going for growth" to his or her weekly e-mail to the global staff, and expects things to just happen. Furthermore, an acute overemphasis on revenue growth will likely shift the company to a position of simple growth over time, which means the company will lag behind its peers in the creation of shareholder value.

Balance is the critical element because a company needs to be both strong *and* lean. Growth strategies and profit strategies are not mutually exclusive, but rather mutually reinforcing. The value builders form a superior investment because they make a solid and efficient business bigger. They strive to get more out of more instead of more out of less. The pursuit of value-building growth does not imply that a growth company can afford to operate inefficiently but rather that a bottom-line focus alone does not exhaust the company's ability to boost its shareholder value. While CEOs must balance growth and profit, the top performers in terms of shareholder value usually tip the scales in favor of growth. They have learned that an obsession with rationalization and capital efficiency may result in corporate amnesia: an inability to remember how to grow. The short-term focus becomes "short-terminal," as companies fall into a profit trap that is difficult to escape. At the other extreme, growth for growth's sake stretches a company too far and eventually leads to diminishing returns on invested capital.

Why does this matter? The underlying principle of standard corporate valuation models is that the value of a company represents the value of all of its expected future cash flow, discounted back to the present. Numerous studies bear out the link between a company's market value and its ability to generate net cash flow. But this raises two obvious questions: Where do these expectations come from, and where will all that cash come from?

As we discussed in the first chapter, companies have two basic options that will help them increase their pile of cash. They get stronger by accelerating growth and leaner by cutting costs and raising efficiency. Getting stronger has a virtually unlimited upside, while the upside on cost cutting is capped. It takes a company only so far. We argue, then, that companies need to balance both approaches, but they must take as much advantage as possible of the unlimited upside which growth offers. CEOs should establish their companies' growth commitments, switch the engine on, and never switch it off. Value builders reach their positions by going after their hidden potential of growth, not by carving the last piece of gristle from the bone.

Figure 2-16 shows how the centers of gravity of Tyco International and Emerson Electric have moved since 1991, again using averages over a three-year period. Both corporations are North American companies that compete globally and have annual revenues in excess of $10 bn. Both have been value growers, both in 1998 and for the entire decade as a whole. Tyco's revenues have quadrupled since 1994 to roughly $17 bn. Its earnings have followed a similar trend.

By the summer of 1999, Tyco traded at a price-to-earnings (P/E) ratio of 40. Its share price had doubled since September 1998 and had increased tenfold since 1994. Emerson, in contrast, bypassed the aggressive pursuit of growth opportunities in order to nurture what might be the longest streak of profitability in U.S. corporate history. Its net earnings had grown at a compound annual rate of 11 percent since the mid-1950s, having risen for a remarkable 160 consecutive quarters. But Emerson Electric traded at a P/E ratio of 20 in summer 1999 and fell back into simple growth as a result.

The substantial difference—representing billions of dollars in market capitalization—stems from Emerson's imbalance between revenue growth and profitability. Tyco had struck a balance between both, while Emerson chained itself to its bottom line and largely ignored its growth potential.

The external topography: How much influence does it have?

Let us assume that a CEO has made the decision to make revenue growth

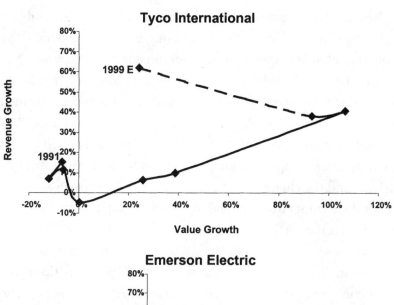

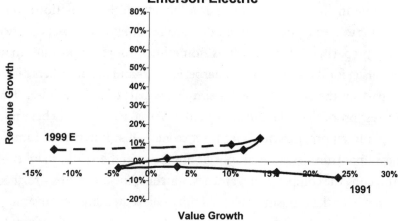

Figure 2-16 The centers of gravity of Tyco International and Emerson Electric.

and profitability strategic co-objectives but with more focus on revenue growth. No matter how well the company, its investors, and its customers accept this decision, it means nothing if the company does not execute it. Tyco CEO Dennis Kozlowski is a firm believer in the unlimited upside, but he also realizes that execution is central to his company's ability to integrate its acquisitions and pursue its internal, organic growth.

The antitrust authorities, as Microsoft can attest, are only the beginning of a long list of things that can prevent this growth. Other easily identifiable suspects come from outside the company. These external factors include competitors, macroeconomic trends and shocks, the sudden emergence of new technologies, and government interference through regulation, taxation, or direct ownership. These external factors constitute the topography of an industry. Much like the merchant sea captains, companies need to know the flow of the currents and the changes in the wind. They need to be aware of the moves their competition is making or planning, and they need to know who is supporting whom.

Even positive changes in the environment can cause harm. An upswing in the economy should be beneficial. Deregulation's very intent is to create opportunities. But as one anonymous observer once said, preparing for the best is sometimes more important than preparing for the worst. And underperformers and profit seekers rarely prepare for the best because it is simply not part of their mindset. The clearest proof that a languishing center of gravity has really begun to seep into an organization's mindset comes when it begins to fumble these opportunities or to simply ignore them. In the 1970s, stability—protecting the company's advantages, watching the downside—reigned supreme. In the e-business age, stability kills. Extending an advantage reigns supreme. Companies allocate and reallocate their resources to gain advantages and then extend them. The real question, then, is: How much does the topography really affect a company's advantages?

Value builders know that the topography—while important—has remarkably little long-term effect on how strongly they grow. Taken as a group, the value builders feel that just 13 percent of their total performance is determined by what goes on outside of their reach. The remaining 87 percent is their own responsibility, for better or for worse. In contrast, companies that are not value builders attribute a startling 44 percent of their performance to topography—that is, a long list of outside factors.

This does not mean that value builders ignore or remain blind to what goes on in the outside world. Take once again the example of Jim Clark and his superyacht *Hyperion*. Clark said that *Hyperion* was designed to let its passengers experience the force of nature and let nature drive them forward. But it is the *Hyperion* that is harnessing nature's forces, not the other way around. The same applies to companies. When asked about a rough time or figures that are below expectations, the non-value-builders respond by saying, "Our market is changing." These companies admit that in their efforts to steer toward ports, they are leaving almost half of their performance to the fate of winds and currents. A value builder, in contrast, declares, "We're changing our market."

These attitudes are reflected in the company's center of gravity because investors have every right to remain skeptical of companies that give half the credit for their success to forces beyond their control and to assign those same forces half the blame when things go wrong. These results also found a strong resonance during discussions with CEOs and top managers throughout the world. As noted in Chapter 1, these top officials said that the reason they do not tap their hidden potential is internal. Their company—not the topography—is at fault.

One group of companies that should face a rough and powerful topography are metals producers that sell commodity products on a global basis. Aluminum producers are particularly vulnerable because that metal is found in abundance nearly everywhere in the world. One expects the fortunes of multinational aluminum producers to be very closely linked to the ups and downs of economic cycles throughout the world. But they are not, as Figure 2-17 shows. The center of gravity of the French aluminum group Pechiney has made some rather wild swings since 1991, prior to its planned merger with Canada's Alcan and Switzerland's algroup. The center of gravity of Alcoa, the world's largest producer, showed a clear upward trend toward value-building growth.

Alcoa attributes its success to the execution of a strategy that clearly sets revenue growth and profitability as strategic co-objectives. The company announced specific revenue targets and used acquisitions both in North America (Alumax and Reynolds) and in Europe (Inespal in Spain, Alumix in Italy) to reach them. The company also pursued organic growth by exploiting new market opportunities, especially in transportation. At the same time, it set specific savings

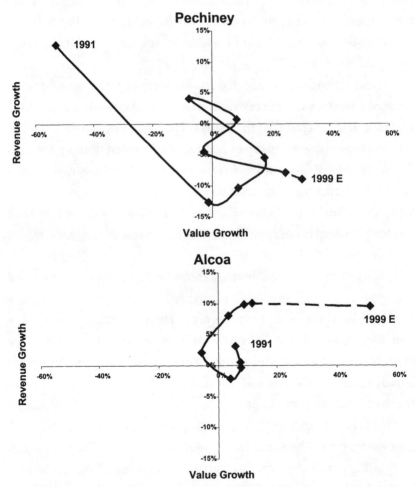

Figure 2-17 Movements of the centers of gravity of France's Pechiney and United States–based Alcoa.

targets and rolled out its Alcoa Business System in an effort to increase efficiency and improve its cost position. The results included revenue increases and improved profitability, despite sharp downturns in aluminum prices. Pechiney obtained a quite different result.

Pechiney

Over the full period of the Growth Study, the French aluminum producer Pechiney ranked as a profit seeker, despite a spiral that led it through all three other regions of the Growth Matrix. Pechiney had expanded through acquisitions. The goal of tapping new resources and promoting growth led the company to purchase the world's largest packaging company, American National Can, in 1988. The success of additional acquisitions at the end of the 1980s and outset of the 1990s helped shift the company away from underperformance and toward the zone of the profit seekers.

After Jean-Pierre Rodier was named CEO in 1994, the company conducted a strategic analysis and realigned its portfolio in order to concentrate on two core areas: aluminum and packaging. The divestiture of underperforming assets helped the company to reduce its debt burden and prepared for privatization, but Pechiney still lagged behind its competitors in overall performance.

In 1996 Pechiney launched an ambitious program called "Challenge" aimed at cost reduction and profit enhancement, which resulted in guide wins in 1997 and 1998. Since mid-1998, Mr. Rodier gave the entire group a new focus to top-line growth, which produced the first visible results in 1999: new sales force dynamics, increased operating margins, better visibility in the industry, and, in the end, early signs of growth in volumes and market value. The planned merger between Pechiney, Alcan, and algroup conjured up growth expectations that were destroyed when the merger-of-three failed due to the concerns of the antitrust commission in Brussels. Pechiney is now faced with the challenge of developing a new growth strategy.

Captain's Log Day 4   **Balance**

Revenue growth and profitability must be strategic co-objectives. Companies which strike a balance between revenue growth and profitability have the best chances to obtain and maintain value-building growth. Balance is key. Overemphasizing either aspect for too long will stunt the company's growth in shareholder value.

Growth is self-induced. The value builders feel that almost all of their performance depends on what they do themselves, not on what goes on around them. Topography—the range of external factors they face—is obviously important. No company can ignore its competitors or escape the reach of government. But the value growers' experience proves that topography is not decisive.

The internal growth arsenal: What do value builders do differently? Value builders have much in common, regardless of their region or industry. The steps they take internally and the areas they foster determine their success. A company's growth arsenal—the tools and levers it uses to outperform its competitors—comprises three categories: growth determination, stakeholder empathy, and an enabling business model. The value builders' success provides a pattern from which other companies can learn, because all companies can apply it in each of these areas.

The individual drivers within these categories represent a mix of hard and soft factors. They address the question, "What is our vision, and how do we pursue it?" as well as the questions, "What do we bring to the market?" and "What makes us unique in the way we do business?" Again, the operative word is *balance*. Value builders pay special attention to all three categories of drivers in their arsenals, without overemphasizing or overreacting. Profit seekers and simple growers reveal an imbalance in one or more areas, either because they have neglected certain opportunities or because they have focused much too heavily on these opportunities. Underperformers show weakness or imbalance in several areas.

The individual drivers are shown in Figure 2-18.

Hennes & Mauritz

The Sweden-based fashion retailer Hennes & Mauritz shows what the balanced use of growth drivers—combined with a philosophy of pushing the envelope—yields in terms of revenue and value growth.

Crucial for the company's success model is stakeholder empathy, with a special focus on customer interaction and superior market intelligence. Throughout the late 1980s and 1990s, though, other growth drivers played a prominent role in the company's expansion.

Starting in 1988, the company built upon what it had learned in its Swedish home market to make a successful entry into the German market. This represented more than simple geographic expansion. Rather, the company leveraged its enabling business model—defined by core competencies in marketing, logistics,

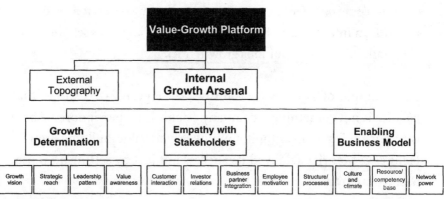

Figure 2-18 The internal growth arsenal has three broad categories, each with four drivers.

and sourcing—in order to make the successful transition to a much larger market.

As geographic expansion rolled on in subsequent years, the company took two steps to ensure that it did not become a victim of its own growth. First, it strengthened its IT infrastructure to cope with anticipated growth. It also made sure that its growth determination never diminished. Management instilled a corporate culture directed at maintaining cost efficiency and fighting complacency.

The only stretch in the nineties when H&M underperformed its peers in shareholder value creation climaxed in 1995. This had little impact, however, on the long-term trend of its center of gravity. This "bump in the road" coincided with a temporary halt in the company's geographic expansion. Balance was restored by paying special attention to stakeholder empathy at this point, especially toward investors. Shareholder confidence was restored in the following year, when the company unveiled plans to expand in France, Finland, and Luxembourg. After years of successful expansion in Europe, the company now plans to open stores in the United States. In March 2000 the H&M stock fell by 30 percent. The cost of expansion had reduced expected profits and the Managing Director Fabian Månsson, who had only come on board in 1998, left the company to start a new job with an Internet firm. His successor, Rolf Erikson, has set out to continue H&M's ambitious growth track.

The example of Hennes & Mauritz (see Figure 2-19) shows that balance is not something a company establishes, then ignores. There is no such thing as an autopilot on the way to value-building growth. Hennes & Mauritz achieved its success not just by setting an initial balance but by restoring that balance quickly and resolutely as soon as deficits became apparent.

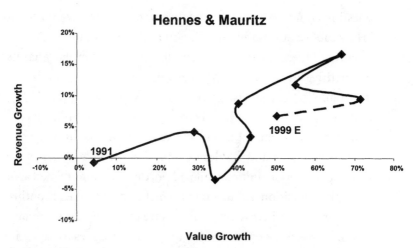

Figure 2-19 The center of gravity of Hennes & Mauritz, 1991 to 1999.

Growth determination as the source of the commitment.

Growth determination covers many bases that are essential to achieve value-building growth. Value builders establish and promote a growth vision, extend their strategic reach, strengthen their leadership structure, and show keen value awareness.

- *Growth vision.* The growth vision must be long term, ambitious, and convincing. It requires a quantitative basis and must have a forceful, compelling, emotional resonance. Though the end product is usually summed up in one or two concise sentences, the creation of a vision requires considerable work before it clearly reflects what the company plans to achieve, based on its capabilities and its opportunities. The most convincing growth visions are not descriptive of a future state of the company but contain a quantitative element that is achievable only if the company truly commits and stretches itself.

- *Strategic reach.* The strategic reach reveals where and how a company plans to turn this vision into reality. It reaches into questions ranging from "What do we want to be in five years?" to "How can we best fulfill our mission to serve customers?" The answers to these questions determine where the company has its competitive advantages, and where and how it will extend its leadership in those areas. It needs to focus on its core set of resources, but also stretch and leverage that core in order to remain ahead. Some value builders accomplish this through extensive research and development in order to take advantage of white space opportunities, while others diversify into related areas through acquisition. At the same time, the value builders continually reexamine themselves to make sure they have the optimal match between the opportunities and their resources to capitalize on them. Value builders have a set of growth initiatives—derived from their strategy—for each year going forward, so that the push and the pressure for growth never ceases.

- *Leadership structure.* New levels of global competition have muddled the leadership role in companies around the world. Commitment, ambition, and drive remain essential qualities for leaders, particularly those pushing a company along a growth path. Tomorrow's leaders must also have a passion for growth. High-growth companies lead the way by seeking out multi-national leaders with cross-functional expertise and a broad range of experience from a variety of industries, hiring different leaders with different skills for different situations. A start-up, for example, needs leaders with an "entrepreneurial" spirit who build the operation from scratch and deal with a wide range of issues—from understanding tax and legal environments to deciding whether to transfer key talent to a new country.

- *Value awareness.* This aspect brings us back to the discussion of strong and lean. Value builders also remain lean because they take advantage of opportunities to lower their costs and improve their efficiency. But they are also aware that the potential for enhancing their returns is greater if they focus primarily on growth—on becoming strong—than on developing tunnel vision toward their restructuring and cost-cutting programs.

Value builders prepare and then execute timely adjustments faster and better than their competitors. Overadjustment, however, causes imbalance, as Australia's Foster's Brewing exemplifies. Its shifts in center of gravity are shown in Figure 2-20. Particular weakness in growth determination prevented the company from breaking out to value-building growth.

Foster's Brewing Group

Australia's Foster's Brewing Group made many strategic moves in the 1990s, but its inherent conflicts and lack of clarity prevented the company from making a clean break from underperformance. The group itself emerged in 1991 from the Elders IXL, whose CEO resigned after unsuccessful acquisitions led to record-setting losses. Reflecting the name change, the company

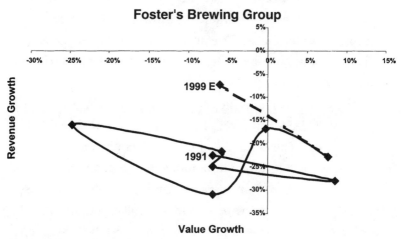

Figure 2-20 The center of gravity of Foster's Brewing Group, 1991 to 1999.

underwent a comprehensive restructuring to prepare itself for a single, focused purpose: to be an international brewing company.

The first stop in Foster's planned globalization effort was the United Kingdom. Ted Kunkel, named CEO in 1992, focused the restructuring process on efficiency enhancement. Through acquisitions and joint ventures, Foster's began to expand both within and beyond Australia. In 1993 the company succeeded in entering the Chinese market, and in 1997 it became the first foreign company to open a brewery in India. These growth efforts failed to yield profitability, however, and major investors began to pull back in 1993 and 1994.

In the second half of the 1990s, Foster's began to divest some of the stakes in breweries that its predecessor company had acquired in the previous decade. In 1995 it sold off its interests in the United Kingdom and, in 1998, its interests in Canada. This marked a deviation from the previous strategy.

After making the decision to enter the wine business, Foster's bought Mildara Blass, one of Australia's leading producers, in 1996 and expanded quickly in the years thereafter. Wine already represented 40 percent of Foster's Brewing Group's revenues by 1997, and this business continued to grow faster than the rest of the company's businesses. Overall, the company posted increases in both revenues and sales since 1997, and by 1999 it came closer to the zero point in the Growth Matrix.

The year 2000 marks the end of the restructuring wave and, driven by a clear-cut vision, the company is now on a steady growth spurt. The e-business initiative is a pivotal factor for Foster's to reach its target of tapping growth potentials in the American and European markets. Aiming at substantial cost advantages, Foster's Brewing Group—in collaboration with 14 leading Australian enterprises—announced in July 2000 that it will set up a cross-industry B2B marketplace.

Empathy with stakeholders: How you bring the world in line with your vision. *Empathy with stakeholders* involves paying attention to all of the constituencies a company touches. A company must be adept at investor relations in order to ensure smooth communication and prevent surprises that shock or spook the market. *Business partner integration* means the company becomes an extended enterprise. Companies accomplish this not only by outsourcing certain parts of their business but also by integrating partners at both ends of the supply chain to encourage innovation, reduce costs, and capitalize on marketing opportunities. Employee motivation requires that a company align its own interests with those of its employees by providing meaningful incentives.

- *Customer interaction.* The customer comes first for value builders at every level of the organization. Serving the company is the sole reason the company even exists. Based on their customer and market intelligence, they constantly seek ways to enhance their interactions with their existing customers and capture new ones. From the company's basic value proposition and its use of creative pricing to its online presence, value builders make the most of their opportunities to understand and interact with customers. The dot.com companies, for instance, conduct business in a one-to-one world in which they and their customers are the sole players. They remove all traces of the intermediaries, they know their customers, and they leverage this information to serve them better. Dell Computer has adopted an exemplary approach to segmentation by aiming different product solutions at a growing range of segments, which now includes schools, small businesses, families, and government organizations.

- *Investor relations.* Companies need to actively manage market expectations. Percy Barnevik, the chairman of Sweden's Investor AB, says that CEOs should spend 20 percent of their time communicating, both within the organization and outside it.

They need to convince the market of their growth vision in the same way that they convince their own staff. They also need to provide enough transparency—backed by timely information—to prevent shocks and surprises. This does not represent, however, a plea to CEOs to make every effort to become the analysts' darling. When true value builders fall out of favor with investors, they usually do so for one of two reasons: Either they are making heavy investments despite perceived negative changes in the market, or they are swallowing and digesting an acquisition. In other words, they are doing exactly the things that make them value builders over the long term. The spirals of Microsoft in this chapter and FedEx in Chapter 4 demonstrate that the companies who stay true to their investments and who continue to return to value-building growth are often in a stronger position than before.

- *Business partner integration.* As companies wrestle with the fundamental questions that determine their strategic reach, they will inevitably face "make-or-buy" decisions. A.T. Kearney's own research in 1999 showed that companies plan to increase significantly the outsourcing of what used to be considered core competencies. These include manufacturing, R&D, and design work. By integrating suppliers in this manner, companies capitalize on the growth side—the larger upside—and not just on the cost savings opportunities that outsourcing usually brings.

  Furthermore, it is universally agreed that the impact of e-business will be much greater on business-to-business relationships than on business-to-consumer relationships. The decision by major companies like automakers Ford and General Motors to shift their procurement to the Internet will create new opportunities to integrate with partners and redefine supply chains.

- *Employee motivation.* The tightness of the U.S. labor market in the last half of the 1990s underscores just how critical it is for companies to maintain satisfied, motivated employees. The model under which employees were offered a secure job and a decent paycheck has been superseded by systems that combine the lure of stock options, the accommodation of lifestyle demands, and the opportunity for further education. People who used to leave their jobs because they "weren't earning enough" now often leave because they "aren't learning enough." This reflects once again the sea change which has replaced stability with advantage.

One company that has demonstrated both growth determination and empathy with their stakeholders is the U.S. financial services company Synovus, which has carved out a strong position as the virtual back office for Internet e-tailers. In 1998 it was rated by *Fortune* magazine as the best company to work for in the United States, then returned as the fifth-best company in the 1999 list. Another company that thrives on these drivers is the Indian software house Infosys.

Infosys

Deregulation in India's software industry paved the way for Infosys to embark on its successful journey to value-building growth. Founded in 1981, the company needed not only a broad strategic reach but also a broad internal and external perspective in order to outperform in an export market already growing by 50 percent per year.

Infosys has long had a reputation for taking care of its employees and its customers. In March 1999 Infosys became the first India-registered company to be listed on a U.S. stock exchange, giving the company an opportunity to expand its employee stock option program (ESOP). It hopes that the NASDAQ listing and the resulting global transparency will help it attract the best talent worldwide. As for customer loyalty, some 90 percent of its sales in the 1999 to 2000 fiscal year are expected to come from current customers. Its efforts to support customers for the Y2K transition were already in full swing in 1996, long before many companies even started to pay attention.

CEO and cofounder N. R. Narayana Murthy views his stakeholders as critical assets with more than a mere intangible value. His view is that the market's valuation of his company allows him to determine the value of human resources, the Infosys brand, the company's intellectual property, and even its customer loyalty. Murthy then focuses on raising the value of the assets on this previously "invisible" balance sheet.

Murthy understands the strategic balancing act between revenue and profitability. "As we move forward, our challenge is to grow while protecting our margins. This requires that we improve our per-capita revenue productivity and contain our costs." The results speak for themselves. The company has achieved steadily rising sales growth through its globalization efforts, and has enjoyed the increasing favor of investors. The company was cited as the "unequivocal stock market favorite" in India in 1998.

The enabling business model makes or breaks the execution. A company's enabling business model provides another integral foundation for success. Even the Internet start-ups, as they mature and grow, will need to devote attention to these areas. Part 3 of this book shows that companies such as Amazon.com—like Apple and FedEx a generation earlier—can make progress for years on vision, customer interaction, and culture alone, coupled with some advantages in information technology. We will argue in Chapter 7 that this basis is not sufficient over the long term because it represents a perilous imbalance. By understanding the need to build their own warehouses in order to deliver the required levels of customer service, Amazon.com has begun to grasp how virtual companies become "real" companies.

Based on our consulting experience, the four critical areas of the business model include the following:

- *Structure, processes, and IT.* A company cannot sustain growth if its internal structures—in terms of organizational structure, processes, and information technology (IT)—do not grow and improve as well. Value builders set milestones—such as absolute size of a division—to tell them when an organizational overhaul is due. They implement processes that encourage and exploit cross-functional communication and knowledge sharing. Parallel to investing in their own R&D, they invest heavily and wisely in IT because it positions them for future growth.

- *Culture and climate.* For growth to endure over the long term, there needs to be an open and progressive culture that fights complacency. The strongest growth rates belong to companies whose internal cultures promote customer service and the ability to meet customers' needs. Empowerment, open communication, and a competitive spirit characterize a value-building culture. One company surveyed said that it rewards people who bring up "ugly issues" and offer solutions, while the U.S. telecommunications giant Sprint pursues growth with what it calls a "bring-it-on" attitude. Finally, the companies follow the motto "what gets measured gets done." Some 84 percent of the value builders tie their incentive systems to growth initiatives, compared with only 22 percent of the others.

- *Resource and competency base.* All CEOs understand the importance of securing key resources to establish their competency in a particular field. The difference lies in how they allocate their resources. Consider, for example, the different ways high-growth companies handle their research and development (R&D) costs during business downturns. When earnings are squeezed, companies that focus on the bottom line almost always force down their budgets, while value builders extend their resources and maintain the same investments in R&D even during hard times. The way in which consumer electronics companies have coped with the transition from analog to digital technology demonstrates the importance of having the right resource profile. While some Japanese manufacturers became complacent and kept milking their analog-based equipment, companies such as the Dutch innovation leader Philips invested serious money in a corps of engineers trained in digital technologies to replace their analog-trained counterparts. This positioned Philips to capture the first fruits of digital television and other devices.

- *Network power.* Successful companies need to establish and foster close relationships with a long list of external parties, from government authorities and trade associations to market analysts and their competitors. Careful attention to these relationships is another hallmark of the value builders. The success of the Star Alliance, a leading global airline alliance, underscores the importance of managing relationships beyond customers and employees. By linking potential competitors such as U.S.-based United Airlines, Brazil's VARIG, Thai Airways, and Germany's Lufthansa, the alliance opens up growth opportunities the individual airlines would be hard-pressed to earn on their own. It gives the airlines' customers access to a seamless, worldwide network. In many industries the establishment of such alliances is extremely critical for long-term survival—as already discussed under "empathy with stakeholders."

One company that has managed to balance all of these elements is Haier. Founded in 1984, it was a child of the emerging e-business age. It combines the vision and energy of a digital company with the tools and infrastructure of a bricks-and-mortar veteran.

Haier

The name "Haier" conjures up an image of Central Europe. Is this perhaps an old East German company? An up-and-coming niche company from Switzerland? Not even close.

Haier is the leading home appliance manufacturer in China. Its growth vision is unmistakably clear: to join the Global Fortune

500 by the year 2010. The company currently at number 500 on the *Fortune* list is U.S. defense and aerospace company Northrup Grumman with revenues of $8.9 bn, which means Haier needs to grow its revenues at slightly more than 30 percent annually between now and 2010 just to pull even on today's list.

The company, the successor of a heavily indebted state-run enterprise, has a charismatic CEO to help implement this growth vision. Zhang Ruimin has made sure that the company is well equipped to secure its leading position in China and expand worldwide. His enablers include technological expertise that rivals the best western white goods manufacturers, a dedicated workforce of around 20,000, and a relatively unbureaucratic approach to decision making, which keeps ideas from logjamming within the organization.

Responding to customer demand, the company has varied the sizes of its appliances to exploit additional niches in otherwise saturated markets. One story about the company's responsiveness concerns a farmer who had continually clogged his washing machine by using it to wash potatoes. The company promptly developed—and successfully marketed—a separate appliance line designed to wash vegetables.

The company's expansion plans include organic growth as well as mergers and acquisitions to establish strong beachheads in major western markets. Its approach to mergers takes a page from the turnaround specialists. The company purchases underperforming firms, then integrates them into the Haier culture. It has also demonstrated an ability to establish and maintain partnerships. The company already has OEM contracts with western firms, but its presence with its own brands will allow it to determine whether its after-sales service—admired and respected within China—has the same resonance among western consumers.

Cynics who dismiss the Haier success story as propaganda or "too good to be true" should take note of how quickly trading relationships change. In 1968, the United States imported 708,000 automobiles from Germany and 170,000 from Japan. In 1980, the United States imported 1,560,000 units from Japan, compared to just 416,000 from Germany. This gave Japanese exporters a compound annual growth rate of 25 percent over a 12-year period, compared with an annual decline of 5 percent per year for German exporters. In this context, Haier's vision looks more realistic after all. And because in the e-business world companies need to think in dog years—one year for them is like seven years for others—Haier will probably tip the scales even sooner.

Applying the internal arsenal: It's time to break some boundaries. The merchant sea captains of old set off to sea and began their exploration and expansion with the same adventurous spirit that pushes the value builders to the edge. Value builders innovate, take risks, and continually expand their borders. This aggressive and adventurous attitude delivers results. A company that tries to live out this adventurous spirit without being balanced will become a shooting star. In contrast, a company that has obtained balance—which is firing on all cylinders—will not be able to resist the allure of aggressively pushing the envelope into new products, new services, and new markets. Value builders consciously define, redefine, and extend markets in which others just participate. Many of the value builders consider this attitude to be the essence of their corporate culture and the foundation for their guiding vision, such as the German software house SAP.

SAP

The goal of the German software group SAP is nothing less than to produce software that will become the industry standard, much as Microsoft has done with *Windows* for the personal computer. Early on, SAP had recognized that client-server applications would erode the position held by mainframe computers. When the market for the mainframe software *R/2* declined in 1992, its successor—*SAP R/3*—was already set for launch.

Software meant to be the industry standard needs to be successful the world over, not just in its home country or continent. An advertising blitz for *R/3* in the United States helped the software become quickly established. In 1996 SAP's sales in the United States had already surpassed those of its competitors in the market for enterprise resource planning (ERP) software, a market that was growing at 20 percent per year. By 1997, the rapid rise had made SAP the world's fourth-largest software company in terms of revenue.

The growth in the first half of the 1990s came largely thanks to geographic expansion. After claiming at one point to have half of the world's 500 largest companies as customers, SAP began in the mid-1990s to attract medium-sized businesses as well. While sales growth reached astronomical highs, SAP continued to invest heavily to improve its programs. The company's revenue rose by 62 percent to DM6 bn in 1997, while net profit rose by 63 percent to DM924 million.

In 1999 the company's revenue growth came in under the more moderate expectation of 30 to 35 percent. The next generation of products is already in the pipeline, however, as SAP is developing a platform for e-business. A bonus system allows employees to benefit from gains in the company's preferred stock and also provides shareholders with a high degree of transparency.

These companies set trends instead of following them. They make and break rules. They show a consistent knack for what philosopher Arthur Koestler referred to as "bisociative thinking," the combination of two previously unrelated elements into something entirely new. They not only become pioneers with groundbreaking innovations, they also introduce a common material to a common application and come up with something "new" like an aluminum can or a paper towel. They take commodities others ignore and turn them into something special. A mere 30 years ago, hardly anyone had ever heard of an aluminum can. Beer and soft drinks came in tin cans. Continuing this pursuit of new market segments and applications, the value builder Alcoa is not just developing processes to make automobile chassis out of aluminum; it has now made "transportation" its fastest-growing business segment.

Value builders break boundaries instead of respecting them. They accomplish this by focusing on various modes of growth, which in essence involve a focus on offering innovative products or product extensions, expanding their geographic reach, and backing those moves with the inherently risky investment they warrant.

Looking more closely at where and how value builders succeed, we found that they "stick to their knitting" by focusing mainly on their existing business rather than on entirely new businesses. They take great risks when they diversify, but they do so concentrically. That means that they buy what they already know and avoid expanding into areas which have little to do with their core. This does not imply, however, that they are one-product or niche companies. They build up ranges of products and services that rely both on breakthrough innovation and incremental improvement, much like Alcoa with aluminum cans and aluminum automobiles.

This helps explain why value builders are companies that avoid cutting back on their research and development in tougher times in order to enhance their bottom line. The chipmaker Intel exemplifies this philosophy. Intel continually ramped up investment in the 1970s and 1980s, with little regard for the revenue and profit the company made in that given year. They gave the impression that they were in business solely to earn the cash they needed to fund even more research. The company took the risk of investing and plowed ahead because people like Andrew Grove and Gordon Moore knew that the development of innovations and product improvements are the real keys to securing future sales growth.

This approach is highly compatible with a strategy of crossing traditional product, customer, and geographical lines. With a stream of both incremental and breakthrough innovations to bring to market, the value builders secure and expand their gains in terms of new customers and new geographic markets. Put simply, they have opportunities that bottom-line-oriented profit seekers or simple growers do not have on a consistent basis.

Value builders also proactively gain geographic coverage rather than just exploiting market growth in their home markets. Value builders have been the pioneers in realizing and capturing the opportunities offered by globalization over the last decade. Their efforts to increase international sales accounted for one-third of their overall growth, and their average annual international sales were 20 percent higher than those of simple growers, and more than four times those of companies with below-average revenue growth. Value builders are the better global companies.

They have also learned that there is a big difference between a company that actively takes risks and a company that—whether it knows it or not—is passively at risk. Passive risk is particularly acute for the simple growers and the profit seekers. Simply put, these are risky, hardly sustainable strategies. Only 26 percent of the profit seekers held their position in that quadrant for two successive five-year periods, as opposed to 48 percent of the value builders. What happened to them? Around 29 percent of the profit seekers migrated to the underperformers, who occupy a hard corner to rise out of. The lesson is clear. A company that continues to squeeze every penny out of existing businesses will see the matrix—and the entire market—pass it by.

Companies that regularly ranked as simple growers took an even harder blow. Only 14 percent of companies who ranked as simple growers held the spot for two successive five-year periods—that is, kept their strategy of all-out revenue growth on track. Well over half of them—some 63 percent—joined the underperformers. A company that expands without consolidating runs the risk that Daewoo currently faces—an underperformance so severe that the entire company itself needs to be dismantled to unlock any remaining value.

The means through which companies grow fall into two broad categories:

- *Organic growers.* Companies have the option of growing internally or organically, which involves relying on in-house resources and building the business from the inside out.
- *External growers.* Companies likewise can grow externally—that is, by merging, acquiring other companies, or establishing joint ventures and other partnerships or alliances.

Most companies employ a mixture of both means. But the organic growers and external growers nonetheless split into distinct ideological camps. The current belief is that successful, growing companies are more acquisitive. Cisco, the record setter in boosting market capitalization, actively acquires companies in order to maintain its technological edge as well as to grow its business. The French automobile component manufacturer Valeo follows a similar strategy, using acquisitions not only to expand its geographic reach but also to enhance the diversity and mix of talent in its extensive R&D base.

The caveat to the active acquirers, however, is to maintain balance and focus on execution. In 1999 A.T. Kearney's own in-depth global survey of mergers and acquisitions revealed that 58 percent of all mergers and acquisitions fail to create above-average shareholder value or meet management expectations. This finding confirms nearly every commentary on mergers and acquisitions since the latest global merger wave began a few years back. The cause for this lack of success is imbalance. Companies that successfully executed their mergers demonstrated unerring commitment to a growth story. Instead of overstressing the synergies to be gained by cost cutting and efficiency improvements, they saw the upside and went for growth. John Reed and Sanford Weill of Citigroup—the company formed by the merger of Citicorp and Travelers Group—put this approach quite succinctly: Take advantage of cross-selling opportunities and reduce costs.

Organic growers feel that a company should rely on its own strengths instead of bringing in someone else's. But the organic growers' argument is irrelevant. Execution is what matters. The value builders disregard the superfluous debate of organic versus external growth and focus instead on getting the job done—by any means. They count superior execution among their core competencies. Value builders achieved on average only 40 percent of growth through external means, that is, by merging, acquiring, or partnering. The remaining 60 percent stemmed from organic, internal growth. The numbers for underperformers, profit seekers, and simple growers are identical.

Mergers and acquisitions boost the overall revenue base quickly, but it takes significant management effort and appropriate post-merger integration to sustain long-term growth. Companies need expertise in communication, risk management, and the resolution of cultural issues. They also need a firm guiding hand at the helm. Likewise, a reliance on organic growth requires a strong sense for making the right bets, backing the right projects, and keeping the projects flowing through the pipeline. In other words, regardless of how the mix between organic and external growth breaks down, execution in both areas is what matters. This is where value builders excel. They succeed in tossing old thinking overboard.

Captain's Log Day 5   Execution matters

Value builders share a common platform for growth. They not only consider themselves responsible for their performance, they pursue it in a similar manner. They balance growth determination, empathy with stakeholders, and an enabling business model. This platform provides a pattern on which other companies can build.

An adventurous spirit !! There is no value-building growth without innovation, risk taking, and geographic expansion. Period.

Execution is what ultimately matters. No matter how balanced and adventurous a company is, it still needs to deliver. The same applies to the way a company grows. Whether it increases revenue by acquisition or organic growth or a mix of both, success or failure ultimately depends on execution, which value builders excel at.

Growth is a process involving the balanced application of all value drivers. But you must still execute. Each position in the matrix—each center of gravity—indicates a significant pattern of behavior and shows when a company is out of balance. Accordingly, this position also marks a specific starting point for the company to begin correcting this imbalance and navigating toward value-building growth. Our experience with underperformers shows that they have clear deficits with regard to vision. Many simply go through a budget-driven strategy ritual under the guidance of their hierarchical, budget-driven leadership. Their lack of strategic focus leaves them with little orientation for finding a way out. The simple growers generate growth momentum, but eventually they become unfocused. Many of them lack strategic discipline. Profit seekers often anchor themselves in the profit trap, where the whole company culture exudes risk aversion and a pervasive controlling mentality. To achieve value-building growth, they need a clean break with this culture. The value builders must keep spiraling up and avoid even the slightest sense of complacency. The longer the company outperforms, the more likely it is that an insidious and destructive mentality of "loosen up" and "we made it" takes hold.

Instead of resting on their laurels, value builders need to apply their upward thinking to actual business situations. Value builders,

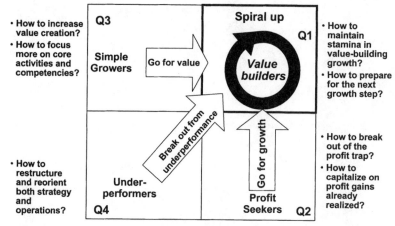

Figure 2-21 Key challenges in the pursuit of value-building growth.

profit seekers, simple growers, and underperformers all face unique strategic challenges. In this chapter we have paved the way for an exploration of the routes to value-building growth. Now it's time to set sail. When we begin to consider the prerequisites for traveling these routes, we arrive at challenges like those in Figure 2-21.

Knowing where to go is one thing. Achieving value-building growth is something else. Part 2, "The Routes to Value-Building Growth," shows how other companies eliminated old ways of thinking, answered key strategic questions, and introduced new approaches on their way to value-building growth. The cases show how each company's center of gravity shifted, how the industry's topography changed, and how the company balanced its growth arsenal and used it to drive forward. The companies avoided generic solutions and acted on their own initiative.

PART 2

The Routes to Value-Building Growth

Breaking out of the profit trap

HOW TO GET "MORE OUT OF MORE" INSTEAD OF "MORE OUT OF LESS"

When the pursuit of higher profit through efficiency gains and cost cutting becomes addictive and repetitive, a company's short-term focus does indeed become short-termism. Success in deriving "more out of less" preoccupies management so strongly that it diverts its attention away from opportunities to get "more out of more." We refer to this kind of thinking as the "profit trap." Companies in the profit trap become complacent and comfortable as they carve out efficiency gains year after year. The word of the controller becomes gospel, which can lead to risk-averse behavior and choke off the investment that is central to developing innovative products and bringing them to market.

The center of gravity of the profit seekers truly reflects their corporate mindset and results directly from a clear imbalance with regard to the growth arsenal. The profit seekers admit that they are risk averse and conservative. They have no clearly defined growth vision. They adopt caretaker strategies instead of expansive ones, feeling that "good" is "good enough." As one division head of a

European packaging company puts it: "We simply don't know how to grow any more. All the systems are on cost control, efficiency, and bottom line. Growth has a connotation of increasing your risk and being negative. So in our company culture, to be on the safe side, we improve our cost position, and then limit our growth initiatives based on the numbers of the previous year, so that we can survive in our organization."

The shifts in a company's center of gravity show clearly when a company has settled into the profit trap. The three-year moving average is anchored in the profit seeker region. Despite sharp movements, the company does not make a sustained breakout into value-building growth. Few profit seekers consider revenue growth to be a priority, and a small handful do not consider it to be a major management issue. Instead, the profit seekers have a knack for identifying and removing internal bottlenecks and have achieved some noteworthy successes. They struggle, however, in identifying and removing barriers to growth.

Dissolving these structural barriers requires a quantum leap away from short-termism. It involves leveraging and stretching the company's core business, which in turn demands a dogged commitment to investments and growth-oriented strategic initiatives that might not show tangible results for a year or two. But most profit seekers find it hard to change their spots. For them, stability still reigns supreme. In contrast to value builders, profit seekers feel that they have a strong exposure to macroeconomic changes and competitive shifts, and attribute more than half of their performance to them.

Empathy with stakeholders is often just as underemphasized as growth determination. The investor relations of the profit seekers remain on the safe side: Just pay the dividend. They often possess strong brand names, but they fail to exploit them because they limit their customer interaction. Their employee motivation is often minimal, especially when an antientrepreneurial environment dominates.

The enabling business model is again based on stability and complacency. The culture is pervaded with the shrinking, confining mentality of cost leadership instead of the expansive, liberating focus on growth. Many companies who have become entrenched profit seekers backtracked from the value-building growth region and have never recovered. Those who made it worked at it for many years before they were able to redirect their center of gravity and regain their balance.

But, as we explained in Chapter 2, getting more out of more—by focusing on the right kind of growth—is the key to achieving the superior returns of a value builder. Profit seekers need to make a clean break from the profit trap—cost cutting and controlling—by aggressively broadening their market and growth orientations. Instead of scrapping their efficiency expertise, they need to balance it by introducing growth as a strategic co-objective with a high priority throughout the organization. They also need to devote much attention to what they can control—what happens in their own extended organization—and become less dependent on external influences. Finally, the company's business model needs to support this new growth orientation. (See Figure 3-1.)

Figure 3-1 Basic changes profit seekers need to make to achieve value-building growth.

This chapter presents two cases that show how companies cope with the profit trap. Hershey Foods, the largest U.S. manufacturer of chocolate and confectionery products, weighed anchor, broke functional bottlenecks, and dissolved structural barriers in the organization. Driven by a clear change in mindset, the company broke out to a position of value-building growth. HBOC, which provides information solutions for the healthcare industry, made a commitment to a narrower service area, then tapped the growth potential hidden within it.

HERSHEY FOODS

What does a company do when it has won the war after years of intense battles? It keeps on fighting, of course.

In the early 1980s the business battles that received the most popular attention came from the so-called Cola Wars. The battlefields—from store shelves to picnic tables, from television screens to business magazines—witnessed an entertaining but deadly serious battle for market leadership between the tradition-bound Coca-Cola and its brash rival Pepsi.

A less-publicized but no less serious war took

> Competitive
> configuration

place simultaneously, however, between two other large companies dedicated to satisfying the sweet tooth of young and old throughout the world. The war between Hershey Foods, which markets what it calls "the Great American Chocolate Bar," and the Mars Corporation, known as the maker of Mars, Snickers, and Twix bars, had also been—and continues to be—in full fury.

Hershey capitalized on some shrewd moves to take market leadership away from Mars in the 1980s. When Mars backed away from an opportunity to have its M&M candies placed in a Steven Spielberg movie, Hershey stepped in with its struggling Reese's Pieces product. *E.T. The Extraterrestrial* soon became the best-selling movie of all time. So many people around the world saw E.T. eat Reese's Pieces instead of M&M's that sales of Reese's Pieces tripled.

At the same time, Hershey acquired companies that were away from its main battlefield, buying, for example, a range of pasta companies. But by the mid-1990s, overall sales growth had begun to slow significantly, and earnings declined as well. Hershey's success in toppling Mars from the top position had left it with a radically different kind of challenge: expanding the lead once they had gained it.

In the early 1990s, Hershey had slipped into the profit trap, where an overemphasis on the bottom line often leads to complacency, which had placed the company at risk for a slip into underperformance. In 1994 and 1995 Hershey's absolute sales growth rates fell to the low single digits, and in 1994 the company's earnings before interest and taxes (EBIT) plunged by 32 percent. These changes are reflected in Hershey's spiral in Figure 3-2, as the company's center of gravity did in fact slide into underperformance in 1994. This position means

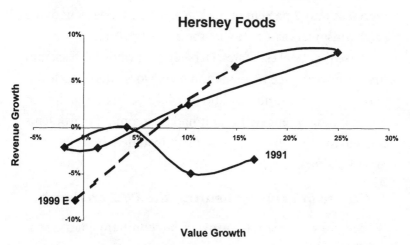

Figure 3-2 Hershey literally made a turnaround and spiraled upward until 1997.

that in three years through 1994, Hershey underperformed its peer group on average.

After 1994, however, Hershey began to spiral up with the true compass setting of a value builder. How did it accomplish this turnaround? The company crafted this change of course through a balanced approach to eliminating bottlenecks, breaking down barriers to growth, and leveraging the company's core competencies in manufacturing and marketing.

Its center of gravity improved after the new CEO, Kenneth L. Wolfe, introduced a new growth determination by making growth and profitability the company's strategic co-objectives.

Growth determination

The company supported this through its innovative category management approach, backed up by an early adoption of information technology to facilitate online interaction with customers and by marketing programs to help retailers sell products, not just stock them. Finally, the company continued to introduce new products that maintained what Hershey calls the "U.S. confectionery industry's tradition" of offering superior customer value. The company noted that private-label sales represent only 2 percent of the U.S. market, a testament to the value consumers associate with the industry's brands.

Based on 1999 estimates, Hershey for a while fell back into underperformance to a position even worse than 1994. But another "turnaround" will be possible because Hershey in February 2000 reported that it had overcome the problems related to the new MIS system it installed in 1999 with extreme difficulties.

Center of gravity: Beating the P&L to death

Hershey needed to grow. The company had spent considerable time getting "more out of less" by adjusting its balance sheet in favor of more leverage and at the same time reducing its cost of capital by three percentage points. It also began weeding out underperforming business lines. But as we stress so often in our book, you cannot cut back and wring out costs forever. As one Hershey manager described it: "We reached a point where the P&L has been beaten to death."

A deeper look at the topography of the confectionery market offers some insight into where Hershey could isolate and pursue some growth opportunities. Hershey may have held a leading market position in chocolate products in the United States, but it still trailed Switzerland's Nestlé—one of the inventors of milk chocolate—on a global basis. Heading abroad and becoming less dependent on North American sales represented a strong possibility.

Internal growth

This topography left chairman and CEO Kenneth L. Wolfe with the challenge of correcting the center of gravity by balancing three forces when he took over in 1993. He needed to make sure that Hershey did not rest on its past successes and succumb to the temptation of complacency. He also needed to strike a balance between breadth of segments and geographic expansion. Wolfe tackled these challenges with an exemplary approach to value-building growth. Hershey began to rely heavily on the interaction among all three parts of his internal arsenal of growth drivers: its enabling business model, its empathy with stakeholders, and its growth determination. Hershey's success in breaking out of the profit trap and recovering from a brush with underperformance shows that the new approach resonates both among candy eaters and investors. (See Figure 3-3.)

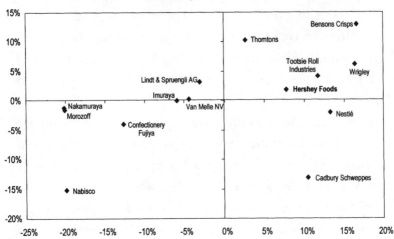

Figure 3-3 Hershey Foods versus global competitors.

Balance: Mixing bits and bytes
with chocolate and peanuts

Information technology

Two crucial elements in Hershey's rise to value-building growth are its dedicated approach to marketing and selling its products and its decision to invest in information technology to create and exploit new opportunities in these areas. Hershey thus has broadened and strengthened a significant competitive advantage: its category management system.

Customer interaction

This system is central to Hershey's relationships with its retail customers. It establishes partnerships with retailers to exchange data and to develop customized programs for marketing efforts and shelf-space management. This holistic approach allows Hershey to offer tailored promotions and to help ensure that the retailer has the right mix of products to sell quickly and profitably.

The system can account for rapid changes at

Market intelligence

both ends. The company not only tracks demand trends for existing products. It can also work new products—which are regularly being brought to market—quickly into the mix and gain immediate and thorough feedback on their performance. As Hershey steps up its international expansion, the system will also provide it a way to keep track and learn the prevailing tastes and preferences in foreign markets.

The company hopes the system will help build its

Investor relationship

brand position among end customers as well and that it will also resonate among analysts and investors. The company began to move slightly away from the chocolate industry tradition of keeping information close to the breast. Although some 30 percent of Hershey shares remain in the hands of passive investors, the company has begun a program of investor relations to help make sure the market knows and understands its goals and how it plans to reach them.

To make this system work and at the same time improve process efficiencies across the company internally, Hershey approved a project in late 1996 to install a company-wide integrated information system. In addition to the internal efficiencies, the company also received at a very early stage an IT infrastructure that proved broadly Y2K compatible.

Extending the competitive advantage of the cate-

e-business

gory management system will represent a key challenge beyond 2000. It shows that a company like Hershey Foods will become more and more dependent on e-business solutions from a business-to-business perspective. It may still be impractical for individual consumers to buy Hershey bars over the Internet, but it is a life-or-death matter that Hershey's remains linked to major retailers like Wal-Mart, which alone counts for 12 percent of the company's sales.

Hershey's successful turnaround since 1994 also offers an especially strong example of a corporate culture that fights complacency. Faced with the opportunity to consolidate its "victory" over Mars by living off the rising trend in chocolate consumption, Hershey set initiatives in motion to keep the pipeline full and to make sure the internal focus remained on "win" instead of "not lose." One such step was the decision to adapt performance-based compensation based on an incentive system. The company aligned its incentive system with the corporate goals of growing market share both domestically and abroad.

> Corporate culture

Hershey knew that in order to grow, it needed to become aware that its domestic battle with Mars and its budding international battle with Nestlé would—and could—never end, no matter how well it performed. This fact became central to Wolfe's leadership philosophy when he became CEO. As one manager warned regarding complacency: "Never believe you're the best—it just makes you a target".

> Market growth

One statistic shows just how large the risk was that Hershey would rest on its laurels. Profit seekers frequently attribute much of their growth to "growing with the market" instead of increasing their market share. According to U.S. Department of Commerce data, the average American's annual consumption of chocolate rose to 24.9 pounds over a 10-year period in the 1990s from 18.3 pounds in the late 1980s. Instead of merely riding this trend, Hershey chose to drive it and capitalize on it.

Research
and
development

When translating its growth goals into specific strategy, Hershey decided not to part with its long-standing emphasis on organic growth as the basis for its expansion and success. In line with a value-building attitude, the company always stressed implementation as the ultimate key factor as it continued to focus heavily on its own research and development efforts to keep its pipeline full.

The company estimates that new products or line extension account for around 60 percent of its growth. The one exception to this commitment to organic growth was the attempt in the 1990s to build up a position in the pasta segment in the United States. This opportunity outside the confectionery market did not live up to the company's ever-stricter performance expectations. In January 1999 it sold 94 percent of its pasta business—including several brands and six manufacturing facilities—to New World Pasta. (See Figure 3-4.)

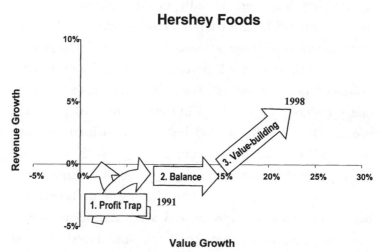

Figure 3-4 Breaking the profit trap does not happen overnight.

Looking beyond 2000

Hershey's past success in achieving value-building growth shows that fundamental changes must be made, both in the short term and long term. By 1998 the company had achieved value-building growth by making some fundamental strategic changes, and by understanding and balancing its internal growth drivers.

A major spark for these changes was the change in leadership in 1993, when Kenneth Wolfe took over as CEO. To keep up this success as a value builder, Wolfe and his team must continue to make fundamental changes to the business. Hershey needs to maintain its newfound internal balance, while continuing to read the topography for clues on where the next opportunities may be found. International expansion remains a wide-open area, as even today Hershey remains an American success story. Sales outside of North America account for just 5 percent of its revenue.

Hershey must also remain on the lookout for unexpected bottlenecks and barriers. One potential bottleneck is the diversity of tastes around the globe. If Hershey ever wants to improve this 5 percent figure and introduce a product pipeline in Europe and Asia as deep as its domestic one, it may face the challenge of funding and fostering such broad research. The second bottleneck—which Hershey shares with many other companies—is skill shortages, especially in the IT area. Some of these may have influenced the development during 1999. Despite a performance-based compensation system and a reputation as one of the "100 Best Companies to Work For," Hershey must remember that it still needs to fight for these scarce resources.

McKESSON HBOC

HBO & Company (HBOC) made such a clear escape from the profit trap that it became an attractive takeover candidate. In 1998 HBOC was bought by McKesson to form what is currently the largest healthcare service company in the United States.

Medicine is an information-intensive business, which means hospitals require powerful, efficient information systems. This simple premise encapsulates the *raison d'être* for HBO & Company, which is now part of the pharmaceutical and healthcare supply management company McKesson.

While this statement sounds rather obvious in today's dot.com world, it represented breakthrough thinking when Walter Huff, Bruce Barrington, and Richard Owens began developing information systems for rural Illinois hospitals in the late 1960s. The trio founded HBO & Company in 1974 with $14,000 in operating capital. The company went public in 1981 to raise money to fund its growing research and development efforts. By the time McKesson bought HBOC in late 1998, the company had annual revenues of $1.2 bn.

Center of gravity: Making the shift away from the profit trap

In the 1980s, HBOC could be best described as a profit seeker, but an atypical one. The difference appeared in its approach to innovation. While the company was unable to match the revenue growth rates of its competitors, it continued the founders' original philosophy of combining strategic mergers and acquisitions with heavy investment in R&D.

Its subsequent high levels of growth could be

*Research
and
development*

attributed to this approach. But at the end of 1989, Huff, the last of the three company founders, left the company. His departure rattled some investors and shifted the company toward underperformance after 10 years of successful growth.

The reorientation phase began after the company hired Charles W. McCall, a former executive at CompuServe, as CEO. McCall prepared the company well for the aggressive expansion course that catapulted HBO into the ranks of the value builders from 1993 onward. One of the first major deals was the merger with HealthQuest, at which point the company changed its name to HBOC. The new company renamed the product lines of its predecessors to reflect the company's new identity and mission of providing health enterprises of all types with flexible, efficient information technology capabilities.

McCall's vision called for HBOC to become the leading company for healthcare management software. "HBOC" should become synonymous with high-quality software and related services, outstanding customer support, innovative thinking, and successful IT solutions. A portfolio realignment and the combination of some business areas also helped reposition the company in the market. (See Figure 3-5.)

Balance: Creating the right environment for execution

While McCall continued the expansion course

*Resource/
competency
base*

laid down by the previous generation of leadership, he took two steps to ensure that HBOC would see the "right kind of growth." In order to realize his vision for HBOC, McCall resisted the temptation to continue on the growth path of the 1980s and

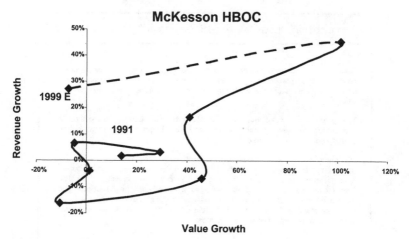

Figure 3-5   The center of gravity of McKesson HBOC, 1991 to 1999.

instead embarked on a path that focused on the company's core business: software for healthcare management. As we discussed in Chapter 2, value builders tend to expand concentrically, growing into related areas.

| Culture and climate |

The company's open culture allowed it to react flexibly to various acquisition opportunities. The personality—the way employees worked together and worked with customers—was underpinned not just by a vision and a mission but by a core set of shared values. This helped McCall turn merger integration into one of the company's core strengths, as he placed particular emphasis on execution. The integration of employees and products in the wake of an acquisition had to function as smoothly as possible.

| Value awareness |

HBOC employees at all levels participated in a bonus program based on growth targets, but McCall also made it clear that every part of the company needed to pull its weight if HBOC was to remain on its successful upward course. This ensured that a culture of "growth for growth's sake" did not take root.

Captain's Log Day 6   Breaking out of the profit trap

Fundamental change is required. Value-building growth is achieved by making fundamental strategic changes and by understanding and balancing internal growth drivers. A change of leadership often provides the spark for such changes.

The process can take time. The breakout to value-building growth cannot happen suddenly, even though the company must begin to make strategic and operational changes immediately.

Vigilance is key. A value builder must continually remain on the lookout for unexpected bottlenecks and barriers if it expects to remain a value builder. One potential bottleneck is the diversity of customers around the globe. The second bottleneck is skill shortages, especially in the IT area. Human resources is a major factor that could limit future growth. Even with a performance-based compensation system and a strong reputation, companies must constantly fight for these resources.

In mid-1998, information first surfaced that a merger might be in the works between HBO and McKesson, a company in North America. The "strategic sale" of HBO to McKesson would help lead to the fulfillment of McCall's vision, both over the short term and the long term. The compatibility of the two partners' product lines was also expected to bring immediate revenue increases due to cross-selling opportunities. The merger would also enable the combined company to enter into e-business, a natural extension of HBOC's capabilities.

Looking beyond 2000

The share price of the combined company, McKesson HBOC, fell sharply in 1999 after the company made downward revisions to previously announced results. Consequently, McKesson HBOC fell back into simple growth. But with its new business unit iMcKesson, the company is apt to grow as the demands on IT continue to rise.

Bringing focus and discipline to good ideas

TRANSFORMING SIMPLE GROWTH INTO VALUE-BUILDING GROWTH

Most simple growers—at their core—have a wealth of good ideas. In many cases, a plethora of good ideas is precisely their problem, as they either underutilize these ideas, or they stretch themselves too thin by pursuing too much simultaneously. They are common in areas experiencing a tremendous wave of economic growth, whether it was Germany in the 1950s, Japan in the 1970s, South Korea in the 1980s or Silicon Valley in the 1990s.

Simple growers are not only run for many years by their founder—such as Dr. Oetker in Germany or Hyundai in Korea—they also have internal cultures strongly influenced by these founders. Although these companies grow rapidly, they encounter problems over the longer term because they are often unable to set up a complete, balanced company with the systems and procedures that characterize value builders.

Companies who want to transform their simple growth into value-building growth need to alter their center of gravity and finally obtain a rounded, complete balance in their growth arsenal. It is not unusual for a simple grower to have a compelling growth vision, a strong leadership team, and an almost altruistic devotion to customer service. But one of the primary conclusions we reached earlier is that growth and profitability need to be pursued as strategic co-objectives.

Simple growers obviously score well on the growth side. They need to strengthen their devotion, however, to the meticulous, nuts-and-bolts activities in which the profit seekers earn their reputation. The simple growers, in this regard, are complementary to the profit seekers. The profit seekers' challenge lies in bringing in enough dollars, euros, and yen at the top line, while the simple growers simply do not make the most of the copious dollars, euros, and yen they actually bring in. Both types of companies are out of balance. For the simple growers, the remedy is a rigorous refocusing on core activities and core competencies, while maintaining growth momentum. (See Figure 4-1.)

Simple growers are not necessarily diversified conglomerates such as the Korean *chaebol*. Even companies such as airline or freight businesses,

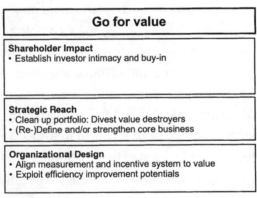

Figure 4-1 Basic steps simple growers need to undertake to "go for value."

which do basically one thing, can still come out of balance. They can overstretch their resources, which leads to unhealthy growth. They seem to be less effective in leveraging their strong customer relationships over the longer term. Or they rely for too long on their superiority in one or two of the drivers in their internal growth arsenal. The latter case describes FedEx, which grew rapidly in the late 1970s and 1980s, then grew up in the 1990s by balancing its approach.

FEDEX

When a company sees a slowdown after a run of simple growth, it faces a special challenge: It must institute a new kind of discipline and a new orientation, even if it means losing the special culture that made the initial growth possible.

In the early 1970s, a young Yale University student named Fred Smith had a dream: overnight delivery—absolutely, positively overnight! And there was more. He was not only convinced that overnight delivery was possible. He believed you could also make money at it.

| Macro impact |

After overcoming enormous resistance to get his small business off the ground, Smith lobbied the U.S. Congress to lift the weight restrictions on airfreight. The resulting "open-sky agreement" enabled FedEx to enter a phase of startling growth.

| Competitive configuration |

Through its brand awareness and customer service in overnight delivery, FedEx matured into a serious competitor to parcel shipment market leader United Parcel Service (UPS) in the 1980s. In the 1990s it finally caught up to its much older competitor as it continued to expand to become an *integrator*, which is a logistics company providing various levels of air and ground shipping services through a vast network. For several years, the two yielded little ground to each other in a head-to-head race that sapped the energy and resources of both companies.

As we said in the last chapter, a company cannot outperform forever. FedEx's revenue growth rates slowed, and the company actually saw its revenues decline in the 1993 to 1994 fiscal year. The downturn is in part attributable to FedEx's struggles to establish a European operation to complement its U.S. operation. The company withdrew from the European domestic delivery market in 1992, and press reports said the company had been losing $1 million per day. The share price began a downward trend that lasted for two years. (See Figure 4-2.)

How did FedEx find its way to value-building growth after the setbacks of the early 1990s? The answer offers insights into the changes that simple growers must make to allow themselves to spiral up.

Center of gravity:
That "federal feeling"

| Leadership pattern and growth vision |

Without the vision and risk taking of Fred Smith, FedEx would never have existed. The charismatic CEO—the only one the company has ever had—lets neither the Cassandra cries of analysts nor stock price fluctuations bother him.

| Investor relations |

Because he knew he would have a hard time convincing potential investors to back his venture, he engaged not one but two consulting firms to test its viability. Both A.T. Kearney and Aerospace Advance Planning were surprised themselves by discovering just how substantial the market for overnight delivery could become.

| Leadership pattern |

It was not only the persistence and perseverance of the CEO that helped keep FedEx going strong. A particular characteristic in its corporate culture

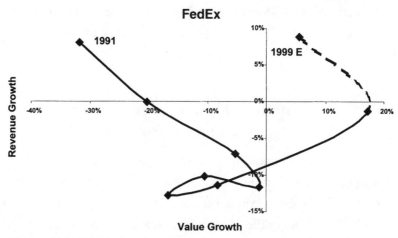

Figure 4-2 FedEx learns to spiral up.

also played a decisive role in bringing the company back to its feet in the mid-1990s after a period of struggle. Since its first days the company has survived many twists and turns thanks largely to the high motivation—some might even say devotion—of the management team.

| Culture and climate |

In the early years it had been the "federal feeling" that melded the employees together. Even today, the philosophy of "People-Service-Profit" is the cornerstone of the corporate culture: If employees are treated with respect and are well compensated, they will readily adopt customer-friendly behavior and an entrepreneurial mindset, which ultimately leads to more profit. To ensure that this continues, FedEx regularly conducts analyses and surveys and uses the results to set goals for employees.

| Employee motivation and customer interaction |

By 1994, the company's nickname had become a synonym for overnight delivery. Phrases such as "Can you FedEx it to me?" had entered standard usage the way "Can you make me a Xerox?" and "Can

95

you hand me a Kleenex?" had done in earlier eras. The company decided to officially adopt the name FedEx as its corporate name.

Balance: A new approach aimed at long-term stability

As demand for international shipments declined in 1992, FedEx responded with a restructuring program in Europe and a strategic reorientation. For the first time in the company's history, the cherished goal of satisfying customers needed to take a backseat—temporarily— to improving efficiency.

Strategic reach

The time had come for FedEx to consider other internal growth drivers to establish balance and prepare for a move to value-building growth. The company succeeded in rein-vigorating itself and resolving its cost and efficiency problems. Following the restructuring, it began with a renewed focus on customer service and profitability. This has resulted in sustained growth in shareholder value since 1995. (See Figure 4-3.)

Internal growth

FedEx can attribute its emergence as a global player to its ability to innovate, expand, and improve its service on an ongoing basis.

In the last half of the 1990s, competition intensified between FedEx and UPS. After its period of efficiency improvements, FedEx resumed its geographic expansion and began to shift its primary focus back to improving customer satisfaction. In cooperation with partners such as SAP and IBM, the company invested in advanced information technology to allow customers to track their shipments on the Internet. Observers predict that the current Internet boom—thanks to the service opportunities as well as to the rise in package ship-

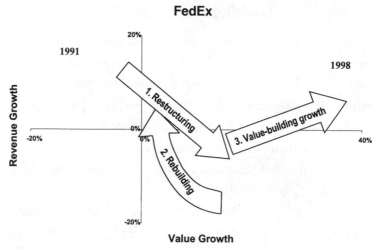

Figure 4-3 FedEx makes the right moves to become a value builder.

ments generated by online shopping—will help FedEx extend its success.

The acquisition of Caliber Systems in 1998
helped put the company's success chances on
even more solid footing. Caliber Systems was
considered UPS's toughest competitor in ground transportation. Caliber's subsidiaries provided the basis for the
diversification of FedEx: RPS, which is now FedEx-Ground,
the second largest shipper of small packages, and Roberts
Express, which is now FedEx-Customer Critical, the world's
largest express trucking company. Viking Freight, a leading
regional trucking company, FedEx-Logistics, and FedEx-
Trade Networks are also under the FedEx banner.

Analysts currently believe that airfreight—the core business of FedEx—will grow sharply in volume terms, but it will
not be as profitable as ground transportation. The focused
diversification of FedEx would then serve to shield the
company against any major downturns.

> *Diversification*

Looking beyond 2000

As the new millennium began, it seemed hardly a day went by without another announcement from FedEx or UPS regarding a new service offering, a repositioning or reorganization. This demonstrates not only how extremely competitive the market for air and ground freight is but also the extent of the opportunities available as consumers step up their online buying and businesses make integrators an intimate part of their supply chains.

In January 2000, the company revealed plans to invest approximately $250 million to build up a home delivery service that will initially serve half of all U.S. customers by spring. The company expects the service to be available throughout the entire United States by 2004.

The stakes for FedEx were also raised when UPS made an initial public offering in late 1999, valued at around $5 bn. This move will allow investors to make direct comparisons when they value the two competitors, and the initial response to the UPS offering was favorable.

The attention and passion surrounding industrial conglomerates—a collection of seemingly unrelated businesses under one corporate umbrella—has certainly diminished the empires of ITT and Gulf + Western, which reached their peak some 30 years ago. Many companies, however, still maintain this style of corporate structure, with widely varying degrees of success.

General Electric, as we mentioned in Chapter 2, began the 1990s as an underperforming conglomerate. Still a conglomerate in businesses ranging from jet engines to home appliances to broadcasting, the company entered the twenty-first century as a model value builder and one of the world's most valuable companies. The Finnish telecommunications giant Nokia (featured in the next chapter), likewise began the decade as an underperforming conglomerate. But under the leadership of Jorma Ollila, the company completed its withdrawal from business such as tires and televisions and became a singularly focused company in terms of product range. Nokia is now the most valuable exchange-listed company in Europe.

In between are companies such as the U.S. industrial and consumer products giant 3M, which is not featured as a separate case in this book. The venerable maker of tens of thousands of individual products in a wide range of segments began the twenty-first century as a profit seeker, exactly in the same area it spent most of the 1990s. Then there are the simple growers we mentioned at the outset of this chapter, especially the Korean *chaebol.*

These examples show that no clear-cut, quantifiable answer exists on how many lines of business or how many product ranges a company should have. But many indicators show that breaking a company apart is the big bang that "releases" the energy to boost shareholder value. The current popularity of tracking stocks illustrates the potential shareholder value that companies carry within themselves. The demand for the IPO of the chipmaker Infineon, which is being spun out of the Siemens industrial group, was so high that the offer was oversubscribed 33 times, unprecedented for German's equity market.

Another German company, Hoechst, has all but finished a Nokia-like transformation from a powerful chemicals powerhouse to a global life sciences company. Even the name "Hoechst" vanished after the company merged with Rhône-Poulenc's life sciences business to form Aventis. The German chemical and pharmaceutical giant Bayer is now asking itself a similar question: Are we better off as a conglomerate?

This section of Chapter 4 will discuss a European conglomerate, Norway's Norsk Hydro, against this backdrop. Norsk Hydro has interests in industries such as aluminum, which have been consolidating rapidly in the past few years. But corporate fusion may make matters only worse at this time, until the company has resolved the question of corporate fission: Would they be better off without some of their businesses?

NORSK HYDRO

Norsk Hydro—a sprawling $13 bn conglomerate with major interests in energy, agriculture, and nonferrous metals—benefited in the early 1990s when it became introspective and made adjustments to its business model. When growth later slowed and the efficiency gains stalled, the company realized a key lesson: Making the necessary adjustments must be an ongoing process, not an ad hoc one.

From its humble roots as a Norwegian fertilizer producer, Norsk Hydro grew over the course of the twentieth century into a global player in fertilizers, oil and gas, aluminum, magnesium, and petrochemicals, while also holding significant positions in areas such as fish farming. The common bond between these diverse sectors is energy. The energy derived from hydroelectric power and from oil and gas fueled Norsk Hydro's growth and became the basis for its diversification.

The heterogeneous core businesses of Norsk Hydro, in which the Norwegian government has a 43.5 percent stake, have something else in common: sensitivity to world market prices for commodities. Norsk Hydro's success is seen as dependent on events beyond its borders and its control. This can have positive effects as well. Rising demand and higher commodity prices helped turn the company's improvement program, launched in 1992, into an overwhelming success. But Norsk Hydro was unable to hold its position among the value builders. The company had barely reached its peak before it began spiraling back, first toward simple growth, then toward underperformance.

Figure 4-4 shows a relatively clear picture of Norsk Hydro's situation in terms of value-building growth. While the contrast does not seem significant, the story is still visible. Norsk Hydro has underperformed its competitors in both metals and oil and gas, and it ranks as a slight underperformer on an overall basis.

Center of gravity: Igniting the growth engine

As economic weakness sent sales and shareholder value tumbling in 1992, Norsk Hydro launched the first broad-based improvement program in its history. After looking outward for four decades as a textbook conglomerate—through geographic expansion and broad diversification—the company decided to look internally and draw on its improvement potential.

> Growth determination and resource base

"Norsk Hydro Plus" catapulted the company into the value-building growth quadrant within three years. The company improved its ability to

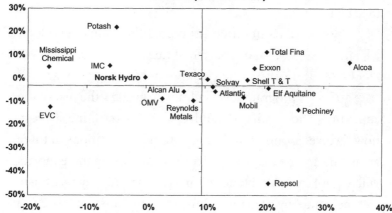

Norsk Hydro versus global competitors
CAGR (1988–1999)

Figure 4-4 Norsk Hydro versus global competitors.

innovate, strengthened its resource management, and raised its efficiency. The group consistently improved its revenue growth relative to its competitors. The measures also helped the group triple its operating profit between 1992 and 1995.

| Employee motivation |

As an additional motivation, the group's management introduced a bonus system for employees in 1995, in order to allow them to share in the success of Norsk Hydro Plus. But the idea of Norsk Hydro Plus had focused solely on operating results and other performance indicators, not revenue growth, even though the revenue gains were strong. In 1996, encouraged by the results of the previous 3 years, the company set a goal of achieving a 15 percent return on capital employed (ROCE) for the next 10 years.

| Macro impact |

But once the efficiencies had been achieved and rewarded by investors, the company lost its momentum. Operating profit stayed on the plateau it first reached in 1995, before declining from those levels. The growth engine has also had little power since 1997, and the conglomerate's growth rates dwindled. The indirect effects of the Asian crisis helped dampen growth even more. (See Figure 4-5.)

| Growth determination |

This situation prompted the company to look inward once again. It turned its sights to growth in 1999, when it announced a long-term growth program set to culminate in 2005, the year of the company's one hundredth anniversary. The resulting strategy now revolves around building strong global positions in three areas: energy, metals, and agriculture. Achieving these targets will require considerable additional change and may eventually call the company's current, slimmer conglomerate structure into question.

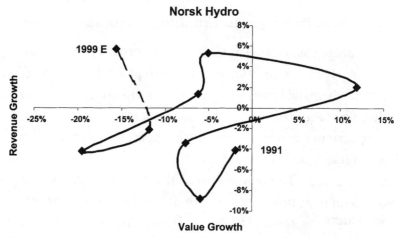

Figure 4-5   Norsk Hydro spirals down from value-building growth.

Norsk Hydro's agriculture business is its largest in terms of revenue, but it also faces overcapacity in the European market. Its sales also fell in 1999. Its other two major pillars—light metals and petroleum—are undergoing global consolidation to such a degree that antitrust authorities in the United States and European Union have threatened to scuttle blockbuster deals such as the three-way merger between Pechiney, Alcan, and algroup (which was cancelled) and BP Amoco's purchase of Atlantic Richfield. Furthermore, Norway is already planning for the day when its petroleum reserves and production decline.

Norsk Hydro has participated in this trend as well, most notably through its acquisition of Saga Petroleum in 1999. The addition of Saga helped boost Norsk Hydro's oil revenues significantly in 1999. Saga also brought access to projects in the United Kingdom, Libya, and Iran, which should help Norsk Hydro toward its goal of doubling energy production to around 800,000 barrels of oil equivalent per day by 2005.

Balance: Driving sustainable, continual change

A balanced approach to the growth drivers is crucial for Norsk Hydro's realization of its growth plans through 2005. Norsk Hydro will need to exploit its internal potential and try to embed a growth-oriented culture as it prunes its portfolio. The current trend leaves the question open: Can Norsk Hydro sustain its position this time?

Empathy with stakeholders

The new motto of the plan through 2005 is profitable growth and value-based management. The Norsk Hydro Plus program from the mid-1990s had proven the company can look inward and make changes. The new program will involve looking inward and outward at the same time. Norsk Hydro will combine growth initiatives with a comprehensive restructuring, including a portfolio realignment to weed out underperforming assets.

Growth determination

The Norsk Hydro Plus initiative had given the group a stronger financial position, which it used to fund organic expansion as well as acquisitions. The agricultural division decided to concentrate on specialty products, then expand its reach beyond Western Europe, where it was a market leader. The company looked in particular for partners in production and marketing in order to serve Western European markets with production out of Eastern European facilities.

In the nonferrous metals division, the company has begun to look for white space opportunities in areas such as automotive, which is considered to have high growth potential for aluminum. A joint venture with the state-owned company Temasik in Singapore was founded to investigate such opportunities.

Looking beyond 2000

Despite its commitment to focus on and expand in three areas, Norsk Hydro remains rather broad relative to its competitors. The world's leading aluminum company, Alcoa, provides a stark contrast. But it is also aggressively pursuing acquisition opportunities in order to meet its goal of doubling revenues to $40 bn by 2004. Its recent diversification into the aerospace and industrial supply markets, via its planned $2.3 bn acquisition of Cordant Technologies, represents more of a deepening of relationships than a move toward conglomeration because Cordant and Alcoa have considerable overlap in their customer bases. In petroleum, the remnants of the old Standard Oil empire such as Exxon, Mobil, Sohio (part of BP), and Amoco are gluing themselves back together in the name of size and synergy. Smaller players such as U.S.-based Phillips Petroleum, meanwhile, have opted for a niche strategy under which they pull back from their downstream operations and dedicate themselves to the upstream areas of exploration and production. In agriculture, Norsk Hydro admits that this area will require significant restructuring.

Captain's Log Day 7   **Simple growers**

Even the best need balance. If a company initially grows thanks to its growth vision and culture, it must balance these two with drivers related to empathy with stakeholders and the enabling business model. Otherwise the growth may not be sustainable over the long term. FedEx's history is legendary. But its rise to a leadership position would not have been secure for the long term had it relied solely on vision and culture and the original business model built around them. Vision and culture themselves require adjustment and renewal as the company expands.

Avoid the profit trap. Restructuring efforts may well result in short-term gains on the equity markets, while efforts to rebuild and reinvest afterward do not. Rebuilding, however, is absolutely essential for a company to become able to spiral up to value-building growth. If the company does not undertake these steps in time, it could easily linger among the profit seekers if not the underperformers.

Shareholder value growth is the yardstick to determine whether the conglomerate strategy is still viable over the long term. As we will discuss in our closing chapter, however, companies such as Norsk Hydro probably don't have the time to wait as things unfold through 2005. In a world where advantage matters and stability kills, the gap between value builders and underperformers will widen dramatically. Furthermore, the comfort zones of profit seeking and simple growth will disappear.

Fighting to break out

HOW TO RESTORE THE CONFIDENCE THAT YOUR STAKEHOLDERS HAVE LOST

In light of market trends leading up to 2000, observers have rarely associated Nokia and Sprint with underperformance. Nokia ranks as the largest company in Europe in terms of market capitalization as it helped fuel the popularity of cellular phones across Europe and the rest of the world. In late 1999, MCI WorldCom planned to purchase the U.S. telecommunications giant Sprint for $115 bn, which no underperformer would have deserved. Even though the merger did not work out, Sprint still is a successful company.

It wasn't always that way. Both of these companies began the 1990s as underperformers, which meant that they lagged behind their competitors over the medium term in revenue growth and value creation. But they saw the fruits of their heavy investments and established strong positions for themselves. Both companies shared—manifested in their own unique ways—a common approach to extract themselves from underperformance. (See Figure 5-1.)

Nokia in particular demonstrates that value-building growth is not just a goal or a target. Rather, it is a philosophy, a way of doing

Break out from underperformance
Growth Vision • Establish clear, quantitative vision focused on profitable growth
Strategic Reach • Set a clear direction refocusing on core; avoid strategy shifts • Clean up portfolio based on growth and profitability
Resource Profile • Realign resources, processes, and systems according to restructuring needs • Redesign the value chain
Leadership Pattern • Establish growth-minded, proactive leadership team • Use motivation of new people to fuel growth

Figure 5-1 Underperformers must initiate change throughout the entire organization.

business, that focuses a company and drives it constantly and rigorously toward superior shareholder value. The traditional pattern for breaking out of underperformance called for a company to stabilize its situation, then return to profit, then begin focusing on growth.

Under value-building growth, the company still repositions its processes and resources, but it also makes growth an immediate and high priority. These steps take place in parallel, not one after the other. Otherwise, it would take years for the company to address its lack of growth initiatives and its empty pipeline. This bruising mindset—similar to that of the profit seekers—demotivates employees and hammers away at their intuitive spirit.

Nokia and Sprint each launched initiatives that were executed in parallel. In other words, they worked on growing the company while rebuilding it at the same time. The reason their centers of gravity first moved to the right, then upward, had more to do with when their initiatives took effect. The fundamental efforts to increase efficiency—that is, to remove organizational bottlenecks and growth barriers—can yield tangible results within 6 to 12 months if pursued aggressively and communicated forcibly. The positive impact on the bottom line follows soon after. At the same time, the companies can begin to put longer-range strategic plans in place, which take longer to unfold but have the effect of a rocket booster when they begin to increase a company's top line.

The spirals of the individual companies reveal the results of this parallel pursuit of short-term adjustments and long-term strategic initiatives. Nokia "moved right" across the matrix, before they "moved up." It has graduated from the ranks of underperformance to the ranks of companies tracing the smooth spirals of a classic value builder. The spiral of Sprint showed a similar lateral movement, before the company experienced a fallback from which it is still recovering. Although Sprint did not maintain the value-building position it achieved in the early 1990s, its case offers lessons in how companies combat the ensuing challenges when they have undertaken considerable investment in any extremely dynamic market.

NOKIA

The Finnish mobile phone giant Nokia exemplifies the belief that "good just isn't good enough," no matter how far you have already progressed. It also demonstrates that a conglomerate— no matter how swollen and unwieldy—can turn itself into a global powerhouse in a hurry.

Nokia is one of the world's clearest examples of how an underperforming company can change its center of gravity, strike a fresh new balance, and accelerate to value-building growth. (See Figure 5-2.)

After witnessing the tremendous growth, especially between 1997 and 1999, it is hard to believe that Nokia actually began the 1990s as a money-losing, overdiversified conglomerate that still made things like tires, computers, cable machinery, and TV picture tubes. Prior to that it even manu-

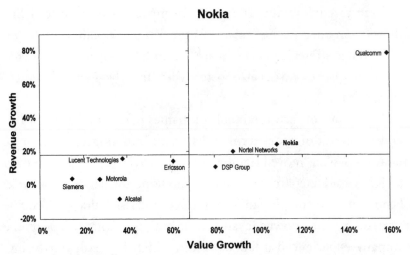

Figure 5-2   Nokia versus competitors.

factured rubber boots. More importantly, Nokia also began the 1990s as a clear underperformer, sharply trailing its competitors in terms of revenue growth and value growth. What changed?

Center of gravity:
Get focused, innovate, and go global

> Leadership pattern
> and strategic reach

If Nokia's history had one major turning point, it came when Jorma Ollila took over as CEO in 1992. In the two years prior to that, Ollila had served as president of one of the Nokia Group's many divisions—the one that made mobile telephones. Ollila quickly made three decisions that focused the company's mindset and resources on telecommunications, with a primary emphasis on wireless. First, he accelerated the company's divestiture of noncore businesses—that is, those that did not relate to mobile phones or telecommunication networks. Second, he ramped up extensive investment in research and development. Finally, he set out to make the more focused and aggressive Nokia Group a truly global business.

He succeeded on all three counts. As late as 1994, when the Nokia group had annual revenues of just over $5 bn, the business groups telecommunications and mobile phones represented only 58 percent of the total. In 1999, Nokia sales grew by 48 percent to $19.7 bn, and telecommunications (now networks) and mobile phones accounted for nearly all of it.

Nokia now ranks as the world's largest manufacturer and marketer of mobile phone handsets. It boosted its global share of the mobile phone market to 26.9 percent in 1999 from 22.9 percent in 1998, according to the company Dataquest. Its top rivals, U.S.-based Motorola and Sweden's Ericsson, saw their shares decline (see Figure 5-3). Observers credit Nokia's meteoric rise in the mobile phone industry to its consistent ability to bring innovative products to market. Compared to rivals, Nokia has a broader and deeper product range and notable strengths in sales, distribution, and marketing.

| Resource and competence base |

The richness of the company's innovation pipeline reflects its commitment to investing in research and development, in which nearly one-third of the company's worldwide staff works. The company's investment in R&D is rising strongly both in absolute and relative terms. It rose by 53 percent—faster than revenue—to over $1.7 bn in 1999. R&D funding now comes to 8.9 percent of revenues.

Nokia's globalization also made further strides in 1999. In 1994 the company still derived 70 percent of its sales in Europe. It has since driven that share down to a shade over 50 percent, after making the United States and China its two largest markets.

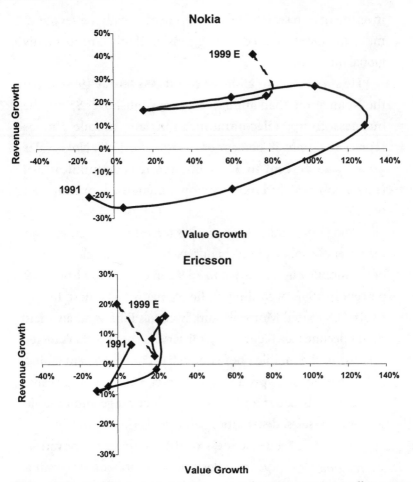

Figure 5-3 Nokia's broad spiral compared to Ericsson's smaller one.

Balance: Mixing strong and lean

The vision of becoming the global leader in wireless communications and telecommunications technology, again, is only implicitly quantitative. It requires the company to grow much faster than a market that is itself experiencing nothing short of a boom. Nokia's success depended heavily on breadth and timing. In the mid-1990s it became the first handset supplier to support all of the world's major cellular standards, and likewise it offered a deep and attractive range of products in each area. Then it continued to match or beat its competitors to the market with more advanced models, attracting both new users and experienced users who were already trading up to a newer model.

The company's sheer size was an advantage as well. Ollila pursued size not only for its scale effects in product development and manufacturing, but for the leverage it gave his company with suppliers. When a bottleneck arises for certain components, being big often means being at the head of the line for the scarce inputs.

Enabling business model

Prior to the divestitures throughout the 1990s, however, the company went through a restructuring process. The company lost a total of $350 million between 1992 and 1994 as Ollila pursued his mission of placing Nokia's only priority on its rapidly growing gems—mobile phones and telecommunications—and selling off the rest. That was the only way for Nokia to introduce the focused research and the customer commitment that we anticipated. Once free to focus on its new core, Nokia became a textbook example of value-building growth. Since 1995, revenues have grown by a compound annual rate of 33 percent per year, and net profit by a compound annual rate of 62 percent through 1999. The company's market capitalization stood at $240 bn in early February, making Nokia one of the world's most valuable corporations.

Business partner integration

In the telecommunications sector, a rich network of alliances is essential, and Nokia is no exception. The company is a member of the Symbian alliance, along with Ericsson, Psion, and Motorola. The alliance is dedicated to developing the next generation of digital mobile telephones. The company also signed an agreement to work with the credit card company Visa to develop secure payment systems usable over the mobile phone.

Looking beyond 2000

Under the slogan "mobile information society," Nokia wants to accelerate its efforts to allow its customers to use their mobile phones to do everything they currently can accomplish with fixed-line phones. The challenge for Nokia is to continue the balance that has ignited its growth over the last five years: a broad and deep product range introduced timely and globally.

The immediate future for Nokia and all of its competitors will involve a wireless application protocol (WAP). The emergence of WAP, and the hardware to support it, marks the first mainstream effort to open up Internet surfing and a range of other communications possibilities to the mobile phone.

Within the next two years, the general packet radio system (GPRS) will introduce a greater bandwidth, which will facilitate the transmission of data in packages and allow customers to be charged by the data received or sent, not by the amount of time they spend online. Customers could remain online 24 hours a day without incurring the charges they would under current systems. The next step beyond GPRS is the universal mobile telephone standard (UMTS), whose data transmission capabilities will far exceed those of fixed lines and would, for example, make videoconferencing via mobile phone a reality.

SPRINT

Sprint had a long and successful rise to value-building growth before its balance became upset and it slipped into the profit trap.

At the peak of its growth in the mid-1990s, the U.S.-based telecommunications company Sprint called itself the company that kept its promises. "We had the vision of the first nation-wide, all-digital fiber-optic network, and we built it," CEO William T. Esrey told shareholders. "We are building the company that will deliver what others are just talking about."

For much of the 1990s, Sprint was a classic value builder. For the period of our Growth Study as a whole, however, Sprint's aggregated average performance lands it in the gray zone where all four quadrants meet, as a slight underperformer.

How could a company slip back toward the crosshairs of the matrix? A look at Sprint's spiral (see Figure 5-4)—which traces the development of its center of gravity over the same period—reveals a clear turning point in 1994. This turning point raises many questions: Did something suddenly change in the mid-1990s? If so, how did Sprint respond to that change? What factors explain Sprint's run of value-building growth up to 1994, and why were these factors no longer suffi-cient to allow Sprint to take yet another step forward?

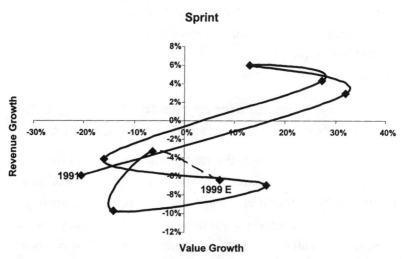

Figure 5-4 Sprint falls back from value growth, 1994 to 1999.

Esrey had much to be happy about as he looked

Competitive
configuration

out across the telecommunications landscape at the end of 1994. While competitors struggled to make the transition from analog to digital technology, Sprint grew steadily between 1986 and 1994 to become the third-largest long-distance carrier in the U.S. market. Its 10 percent market share placed it behind MCI with 20 percent but still well behind AT&T with a 60 percent share of the market. Changes in the global telecommunications market—thanks in part to relaxation of government regulation—helped open up domestic and international markets in the first half of the 1990s.

By the middle of the decade, Sprint stood at a

Macro impact

crossroads in its development, as its spiral shows. It stood on the threshold of an even stronger move upward, but it also faced the risk of experiencing a fallback. Companies had already begun jockeying for positions ahead of the further deregulation of the U.S. telecommunications market in 1996, which would mark the beginning of the real race among telecom carriers. How would this deregulation—which had the potential to make far-reaching changes in the competitive environment—influence Sprint's impressive stretch of growth?

Center of gravity:
A commitment to remaining one step ahead

Through the mid-1990s, Sprint had built its

Growth
determination

growth through investment and innovation in lucrative business areas, as well as through mergers and alliances. The company had a presence in all existing market segments by 1992, then set its sights on global expansion after a restructuring period in

1993, in an effort to find new growth markets. Long-distance service formed the core of the company's $17 bn in annual revenues, but the company also drew significant revenues in local service—its original business—as well as in mobile services (Sprint PCS) and in directory publishing.

When it came to introducing new technologies, Sprint was always one step ahead. In 1986 Sprint became the first carrier to have a complete digital fiber-optic network spanning the continental United States. In terms of quality and customer orientation, Sprint lived up to its claim of "setting the standards by which others are judged." This served as the company's motto in 1993.

| Customer interaction and resource base |

Sprint focused its strategy on investing today in the technology of tomorrow. Much like the chipmaker Intel, which built greenfield factories before it even needed them, Sprint wanted to be ready to meet the demand for new services the moment it arrived, without having to add capacity or play catchup. In this regard, Sprint viewed the developments in information technology not as a threat but rather as an opportunity to be seized and exploited.

| Strategic reach |

The company also succeeded in communicating this strategy to customers and investors. Shareholders acknowledged Sprint's commitment as well as its results. Additional investments in the first half of the 1990s sought to prepare the company for the anticipated convergence of audio, video, and data transmission, which would require a fast and efficient network.

| Empathy with stakeholders |

Finally, Sprint benefited from its image as a technology leader, which is linked to the company's name. The brand name survived several mergers and acquisitions as the company was built up. It

| Customer interaction |

came into existence in its most familiar form in 1989, when United Telecommunications bought a majority stake in U.S. Sprint. This merger combined innovative strength with a recognized brand name, which led to the logical decision to rename the new company as Sprint Corporation in 1991.

Under Esrey's leadership, management emphasized

| Culture |

long-range planning. A growth-oriented culture that encouraged open communication helped the company realize its long-term goals. The long-range planning, as mentioned above, would inevitably focus on convergence, as the boundaries between local and long-distance operators, between fixed and mobile services and the Internet, and even between hardware and content suppliers would blur. The company felt it needed to be able to offer this kind of one-stop shopping.

Balance: Trying to go two steps ahead instead of one

Prior to the deregulation in the United States in 1996, Sprint took two strategic steps designed to limit downside risk and to give the company an even broader base for future growth. As we pointed out in Chapter 2, value builders often migrate away from their positions temporarily for one of two reasons: Either they are investing heavily or they are digesting a large merger or acquisition. In Sprint's case, the investment load—all in the interest of convergence and one-stop shopping—had not paid its full dividends.

First, the company invested in so-called personal communications systems (PCSs), and it took an interest in the joint venture GlobalOne along with France Télécom and Germany's Deutsche Telekom. The investment in a nationwide wireless network—the first ever in the United States—would be the cornerstone of the PCS market and would fit with Sprint's strategy of remaining one step ahead of its competition in terms of technology. In a joint venture with three cable companies, Sprint PCS offered mobile, local, and long-distance calling and cable television in packages. Sprint's profit situation indeed improved—before restructuring changes—but investors remained skeptical about the venture and its growth prospects.

Sprint later issued a tracking stock for the PCS unit, but the company's results in the third quarter of 1999 are symptomatic of the uphill battle Sprint is facing in establishing the network. While the number of customers rose by 87 percent to 720,000, PCS posted a loss of $615 million in the quarter alone. The losses have come at a time when Sprint is also facing pricing pressure in the long-distance business and is trying to launch its ION service, which combines telephone, Internet, and videoconferencing services.

In January 1996 Sprint unveiled a joint venture called GlobalOne with France Télécom and Deutsche Telekom in January 1996. The optimism of investors at that time was short lived, however. The anticipated boost in sales did not meet expectations, and GlobalOne required an enormous startup investment while failing to turn a profit.

Neither PCS nor GlobalOne brought Sprint the success it had hoped for. After MCI, still the number 2 long-distance carrier in the United States, was purchased by WorldCom in 1997, rumors began to circulate in early 1998 that Sprint would be ripe for a takeover. The company fended off the rumors and began a new restructuring program, coupled with additional investments in next-generation technologies. The company could not, however, reverse the setbacks from PCS and GlobalOne.

Captain's Log Day 8   Underperformers

There are no lost causes. If a company's performance situation looks bleak, it needs to break with long-standing traditions, back its winners, and make a fresh start toward value-building growth.

Don't overcompensate. Companies that take things one step at a time in their efforts to establish or regain balance have taken the right approach. It does not make sense to compensate for the previous performance all at once.

At the end of 1999 Sprint finally succumbed to a takeover—from MCI WorldCom. In what was planned to be the largest acquisition in history ($115 bn), Sprint would have ceased to exist as a separate entity but would have lived on in spirit, while the Sprint PCS tracking stock went up over 400 percent in two years. In July 2000 it became clear that the merger could not become reality for antitrust reasons. As a result, Sprint is released into independence again. But the path of consolidation in the telecommunications industry continues.

Extending the advantage

IMPROVING AND EXTENDING VALUE-BUILDING GROWTH: THE MOST VEXING CHALLENGE OF ALL

What happens to the companies that have a tradition of value-building growth? All value builders will eventually face a situation in which they spiral down. You cannot outperform forever, even if you are like Microsoft or Sprint in that you have a robust internal balance.

Some value builders such as Microsoft temporarily leave the upper right region of the Growth Matrix during periods of heavy investment or merger integration. Other value builders such as Sprint, discussed in the previous chapter, seem to apply slower efforts to return to value-building growth.

The two real issues, then, are how to manage or delay the migration away from value-building growth and how to return to it as quickly as possible (see Figure 6-1).

One exception to the fall-back rule, at least through the 1990s, was a media company based in the southwestern United States. An investment of $1000 in Clear Channel Communications at the beginning of

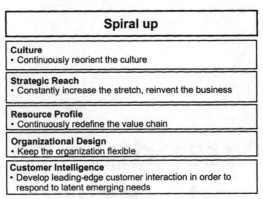

Spiral up
Culture • Continuously reorient the culture
Strategic Reach • Constantly increase the stretch, reinvent the business
Resource Profile • Continuously redefine the value chain
Organizational Design • Keep the organization flexible
Customer Intelligence • Develop leading-edge customer interaction in order to respond to latent emerging needs

Figure 6-1   How to remain a value builder.

1992 would have been worth over $70,000 by the end of 1999—not quite Cisco-esque, but enviable nonetheless.

CLEAR CHANNEL COMMUNICATIONS

This media company is a rarity. It has ranked as a value builder every year since 1988 and shows no signs of slowing down. Clear Channel demonstrates that the secret of growth lies neither in organic growth nor in acquisitions but rather in how you execute.

Just like Sam Walton's first discount department store in rural Arkansas or the first drive-up restaurant of the McDonald's brothers in California, the success story of Clear Channel Communications begins with the purchase of something rather mundane: an FM radio station in San Antonio, Texas, in 1972.

The topography of radio in the United States has changed considerably over the last 25 years, thanks to demographic shifts, technological development, and deregulation meant to encourage competition.

Struggling FM radio stations were not uncommon in 1972, when Lowry Mays and B. J. (Red) McCombs bought their first radio station in San Antonio. AM radio stations—many of which could be heard throughout the world on clear nights—still dominated most markets. Most cars at that time had no FM radios, and most FM stations played "alternative" or "underground rock and roll." (See Figure 6-2.)

FM would soon grow up, however, and Clear Channel would grow along with it. The company and its radio stations profited as yesterday's "underground" and "alternative" rock and roll of the Baby Boom generation became a staple of mainstream radio in a variety of formats, from "classic rock" to "adult contemporary" to "easy listening." These formats attracted advertisers who could use radio to target a specific segment of this consumer-oriented generation.

Technological advancements in stereo recording and audio equipment became a boon for FM as well, as FM could play sophisticated recordings without the static and scratchiness heard on AM radio broadcasts.

The biggest boost for Clear Channel came in 1996, when the Telecommunications Act—the same act that became a turning point for Sprint—also eased restrictions on ownership of radio stations. Companies that could previously own

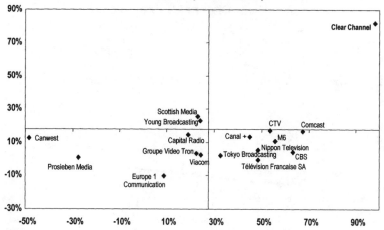

Figure 6-2 Clear Channel versus the competition, 1988 to 1999.

no more than seven FM radio stations and seven AM stations in the entire country could now own that many in one single metropolitan market. While this restriction had already been relaxed somewhat, prior to the enactment of the reforms, the Telecommunications Act of 1996 marked the first official acknowledgment of the change.

The combination of these three changes set the stage for Clear Channel's continued growth over the last four years. When it completes its $56 bn merger with AMFM, Inc. by September 2000, the combined companies will create the world's largest out-of-home media company. Already today, Clear Channel Communications operates 824 radio stations, 19 television stations in the United States, and 550,000 outdoor advertising displays in 32 countries, and it will have a market capitalization of around $45 bn. (See Figure 6-3.)

Center of gravity: Knowing your business

For all the discussion about technology and musical tastes, however, Clear Channel sees itself neither as a technology company nor as a provider of music. It is a "medium"

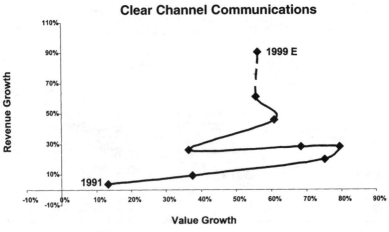

Figure 6-3 Clear Channel spirals up with no migration in sight.

in the truest sense of the word, a go-between for advertisers and their target audiences. "Since our inception, we have focused on helping our clients distribute their marketing messages in the most efficient ways possible," the company says.

Clear Channel feels that the basic idea of finding ways

| Strategic reach |

for advertisers to sell more products and services is a universal theme. This has driven the company abroad in search of acquisition opportunities. The company now derives 13 percent of its revenues outside of the United States. The company's geographic expansion began in earnest with the purchase of a 50 percent stake in Australian Radio Network (ARN) in 1995. Further purchases in Australia and New Zealand followed. In 1999 alone the company bought outdoor advertising properties in Italy, Switzerland, and Poland to broaden its penetration into Europe.

Balance: Execute, execute, execute

Clear Channel executes this idea by creating

| Growth determination |

bundling opportunities for its advertising customers. Its extensive market research leads it to invest in multiple outlets in markets with the highest growth potential. The company markets this palette of advertising opportunities aggressively, with a do-whatever-it-takes approach to attracting key accounts. When one auto dealership initially hesitated to commit, Clear Channel agreed to have its local station broadcast directly from

| Customer interaction |

the dealership on a weekend to demonstrate the company's own commitment to helping its clients sell more products and services.

Clear Channel enhances its understanding of

| Enabling business reach |

local markets by maintaining a decentralized and flexible organizational structure. This provides individual managers with consider-

125

<table>
<tr><td>*Employee motivation*</td></tr>
</table>

able independence and reinforces the company's entrepreneurial culture. Managers also know that their level of compensation is in their own hands. Their pay is based in part on the performance of the broadcast properties in their area.

Clustering can take place not only locally but also at a regional or national level. Despite the company's decentralized structure, it is still well positioned to offer larger companies a broader range of advertising options. This turns the company's extensive network into a competitive advantage. While this national reach is nothing new in television broadcasting, it did not really exist in radio prior to 1996 because of government regulations.

Assembling this network required mergers and acquisitions. Taking advantage of looser regulation prior to the Telecommunications Act of 1996, Clear Channel acquired 60 radio stations between 1992 and 1996. In 1999, it concluded its largest deal yet, acquiring AMFM. These acquisitions have driven Clear Channel's net revenues from $178 million in 1994 to $1.35 bn in 1998, an increase of 650 percent in four years. (See Figure 6-4.)

How does Clear Channel keep pace with these acquisitions and rapid growth? The company relies on its experience in executing mergers and its seasoned management team. Lowry Mays, the cofounder of the company, is still CEO. Second, the company has a strict cost focus, which wrings out efficiency potential in an acquisition, coupled with a growth-oriented focus, which involves extensive knowledge transfer and rapid integration into the Clear Channel network.

Some companies have realized that there are different degrees of value-building growth. Like the example of Tyco International and Emerson Electric in Chapter 2, companies can be value builders

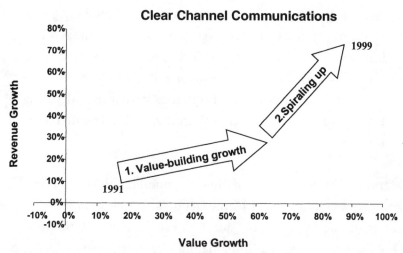

Figure 6-4 Where will the spiral for Clear Channel end?

despite wide discrepancies in their performance. What counts is outperforming the industry average. In the global retail industry, the ranks of the value builders are even more crowded and the competition more intense.

WAL-MART'S CHALLENGERS: HOME DEPOT, AHOLD, AND CARREFOUR

Being a value builder still may not be good enough if your current or future rival is named Wal-Mart. Home Depot, Carrefour, and Ahold are all confronting the challenge head on.

Even among value builders there can be considerable differentiation, as in the examples of Tyco International and Emerson Electric discussed in Chapter 2. Both companies are value builders, but Tyco's aggressive and successful acquisition strategy has helped it achieve a much better position than its relatively conservative counterpart.

The global retail sector also has its share of strong performers, as we show in Figure 6-5. The Dutch food retailing group Ahold and the French general retailing group Carrefour and its merger partner Promodès rank as value builders. Ahold continually sets and achieves ambitious revenue growth targets while maintaining firm control of its operations. Carrefour and Promodès have also had strong runs of value-building growth in the 1990s, despite recent fallbacks.

But the undisputed value-building champion in this sector is the U.S. hardware retailing pioneer Home Depot, nearly alone at the top right corner of the matrix. The spiral shown in Figure 6-6, alongside Ahold's, demonstrates a fundamental reason that Home Depot has been such a strong outperformer: It has never stopped growing. Home Depot's performance over the last decade demonstrates that the centers of gravity of the two European companies still have room to move even further upward (see Figure 6-7). At the same time, all of these companies compete in various degrees with Wal-Mart, the world's largest retailer with over $160 bn in annual revenues. The Wal-

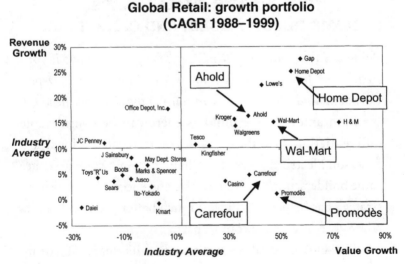

Figure 6-5 The retail sector and its value builders.

128

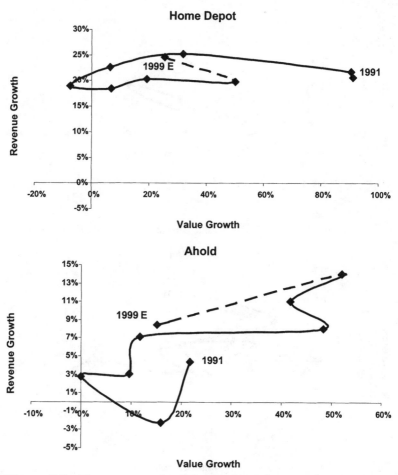

Figure 6-6 The movements of the centers of gravity for Ahold and Home Depot.

Mart superstore model in the United States is really the combination of three separate full-size stores under one roof: a general merchandising section (the Carrefour/Promodès strength), a food and groceries section (the Ahold strength), and a home and garden center (the Home Depot strength). Altogether, in terms of sales, Wal-Mart is as large as the three other groups combined. The real survival test for these value builders has already begun, as each expands into the other's territory, largely through acquisition.

129

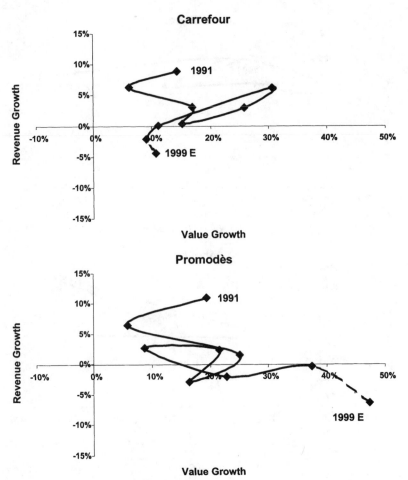

Figure 6-7 The movements of the centers of gravity of French firms Carrefour and Promodès.

Home Depot is still the category leader in retail hardware in the United States, with annual sales of $38 bn and a market capitalization of $150 bn. It is the least global of the challengers, with absolutely no presence in Asia or Europe. But it sets the tone in terms of service. One cornerstone of the company's success is its emphasis on *customer interaction* in the truest sense of the words. Aimed primarily at the do-it-yourself market, the company offers a large selection of products in a warehouse-style format, with specialized staff and even training classes for home repair and renovation. The product mix itself is largely driven by customer feedback and customer suggestions, to ensure that Home Depot continues to deliver what its market wants.

Unlike Toys "R" Us, another pioneering category killer, Home Depot is in a constant state of renewal. Stores are continually upgraded and product offerings culled to offer a compelling buying and learning environment. And like Wal-Mart, the only U.S. retailer with higher sales than Home Depot, the company applies tremendous pressure on its suppliers to maintain its low-pricing policies. While the term *hardware* commonly suggests images of hammers and nails, Home Depot has broadened its range to cover even more aspects of home renovation. For example, it has quickly become the second-largest customer for General Electric's appliances division, trailing only Sears. This gives the company considerable clout.

As competitors responded to Home Depot's redefinition of the market, the company experienced a period in which it pursued new initiatives and ideas in other areas to keep growth strong. Nonetheless, its share price performance lagged that of other retailers, as is often the case when a strong company enters a period of redirection or heavy investment. The company's return to a position of value-building growth—which it still occupies today—was accomplished in part through another wave of geographic expansion, this time beyond the U.S. borders to include Canada and South America.

Ahold has focused much more strongly on geographic expansion and has recently built up strong positions on Wal-Mart's home turf in the United States, where it owns Stop & Shop in the New England states and the Giant chain in the mid-Atlantic region. The Dutch-based group now achieves half of its roughly $40 bn in annual sales in the United States, and less than $2 bn in its home country.

The group's focus on food retailing became sharper after it divested its restaurant holdings in 1989. But the sharp upward trend—mirrored in the company's center of gravity spiral—came after CEO Cees van der Hoeven took control in 1992. He laid out a clear quantitative goal for the group: Sales and profits were to be doubled by 1997. The group met this target via expansion throughout Europe and then in the United States. Like its European acquisitions, the targets in the United States were chosen largely for their regional strength. Stop & Shop is basically only present in New England, where it is a market leader, while Giant is a leading regional chain serving the mid-Atlantic area.

The merger of Carrefour and Promodès brought together two complementary companies with a combined strength in international expansion in both developed and developing companies. With operations in 26 countries, it has the largest international range of the Wal-Mart challengers, and therefore it has extensive practical experience in flexibly and pragmatically handling the cultural, competitive, and cost issues that inevitably arise in cross-border expansion. Prior to the merger, Carrefour made roughly 30 percent of its sales outside Europe.

In their home markets, however, they faced a unique constraint: a ban on the construction of additional hypermarkets. The companies could generate growth in France only by combining efficiency improvements and acquisition, which is exactly the route the two companies chose. Their merger also forms a formidable bulwark against Wal-Mart and Ahold, which are also forbidden from building greenfield sites and can enter France only via the acquisition of an existing chain.

Each of the challengers, as well as Wal-Mart, faces some critical decisions in the near term. Carrefour may have the strength to give Wal-Mart a hard time in Europe, but it has no U.S. presence. Ahold's proven approach of careful, targeted acquisitions may leave it isolated if it does not move quickly enough to consolidate its position. Wal-Mart has bought its way into the United Kingdom by buying Asda. It has also entered Germany by purchasing a chain of Spar stores, but it faces a much more confining environment—in terms of opening hours, union regulations, and competition laws—than it contends with in the United States. Home Depot could follow Wal-Mart's lead and make a large acquisition in order to enter Europe's robust and competitive do-it-yourself market.

No matter who wins this battle, only one outcome is certain: polarization. The comfort zones of profit seeking and simple growth will disappear as the value builders continue to expand, renew themselves, and take advantage of new opportunities. As we will discuss in Chapter 8, this polarization is not limited to just retailers. It affects all companies, which underscores the point that advantage reigns supreme in today's business environment. Stability alone will leave the company dead in the water.

PART 3

The Future of Growth

The shape of today

FACING THE DOT.COM CHALLENGE: GROW UP OR FOLD UP

Most people nowadays don't need data on productivity gains or the blessing of Alan Greenspan to know that the new economy and its digital marketplace—fueled by the use of information technology—really exist. The volume of e-business by 2001 is now projected to run in the trillions of dollars, helped by announcements that Ford and General Motors will each shift tens of billions of dollars in procurement to the Internet. They also plan to go beyond just meeting their own needs. Already the largest consumers of domestically produced steel, the companies feel they can leverage this position and use their networks to buy steel for their suppliers or other third parties.

Other companies now spend millions of dollars in online auctions in a matter of hours, a development that will eliminate printed catalogs and price lists, and eventually erode the importance of trade fairs.

It comes as no surprise, then, when top managers all over the world—from Stockholm to San Francisco, from Goa, India, to Frankfurt, Germany—regularly ask the same question after a discussion about value-building growth: "Value-building growth may be a target

"It's not just me, Dad. Amazon.com has never made a cent, either."

for bricks-and-mortar businesses, but what would you tell a company like Yahoo! or Amazon?"

The answer is quite simple. The insights into value-building growth apply to a traditional steel manufacturer managed by a 55-year-old CEO as well as to an Internet company run by a Generation Xer. No matter what ship is required or what waters are traversed, the model of balance, especially for growth drivers, is timeless and universal. The growth drivers introduced in Chapter 2 also provide a means to understand whether young Internet companies should be as highly prized by investors and what these companies need to do in order to survive as long and as prosperously as the companies we described in Chapter 3. In this respect, the growth drivers expand on what securities traders and investment analysts used to refer to as "corporate fundamentals." However, they add a breadth and depth that go beyond the old fundamentals, which focused more narrowly on financial strength, management depth, and market position. The "complete equation" of the growth drivers allows valid and insightful comparisons among bricks-and-mortar companies, the new breed of digital companies, and those bricks-and-mortar companies who already have embraced e-business.

Respected publications such as the *Economist* have carried the torch of "irrational exuberance" ever since U.S. Federal Reserve Chairman Alan Greenspan uttered those words a few years ago, when the Dow Jones Industrial Average was at roughly half the level it is today. The claim is that Internet shares are wildly overvalued, that their price-to-earnings ratios are unrealistic even if their performance improves dramatically, and that the share prices will inevitably fall, if not crash land. Even more troubling are the fluctuations in share prices. On one single day in December 1999, shares in Yahoo! rose by 20 percent in one single day. It is not unusual for a company like e*Trade or Ameritrade to gain or lose a significant percentage of its value in the time it takes to read this paragraph.

As Yahoo! founder Jerry Yang said in a *Wall Street Journal* interview in late 1999, dot.com companies run a severe risk of becoming out of balance because they lack the infrastructure and the resources to support their growth determination and promises of customer service. "You can buy a lot of companies with that market cap, but . . . if you want to build a Yahoo! product that is heart and soul, flesh and blood Yahoo!, it takes management time, which is very underresourced; it takes engineering time, which is nonexistent; and it takes marketing resources."

The list of faltering dot.com companies has grown for precisely those reasons. Recent examples include the online software seller Beyond.com and the e-tailer Value America. The latter company announced during the 1999 Christmas holidays that it would lay off half of its staff in the midst of a record-setting shopping season. Meanwhile, the company Amazon.com has still not turned a group profit, but it has at least never had a decline in revenue, nor has it ever stopped investing in the IT infrastructure and the distribution warehouses it needs to fulfill its obligations to customers. Despite the hype and the promise, none of these companies will be able to sustain value-building growth over a period of years without doing exactly what successful bricks-and-mortar companies have done before them. They need to make revenue growth and profitability mutually reinforcing co-objectives, which means becoming both strong and lean. They also need to achieve balance in terms of growth determination, empathy with stakeholders, and an enabling business model.

A closer examination of these balance issues—strategic objectives and drivers—shows that the emergence of e-business has thrown most companies off balance and cleaved them into two distinct sets. Gathering all the positive headlines are the dot.coms, with their strong growth visions, innovative products, new forms of customer relations, but often with their very underdeveloped supporting processes and systems and a chronic lack of cost awareness. These companies thrive almost entirely on their growth determination. They successfully articulate their growth visions and their strategies to make them a reality. Their progressive approaches to leadership and the almost irresistible lure of stock options secure them talented, motivated employees as well as goodwill with investors. Combine these elements with an entrepreneurial spirit and a growth mindset, and you have captured the essence of these companies' success.

Just as with the companies we discussed in the previous chapters, the dot.com companies have their share of winners and losers, as the Growth Matrix in Figure 7-1 shows. Because many of these companies have existed only for a few years, their centers of gravity have been determined based on quarterly growth rates instead of annual growth rates. The spirals of the individual companies follow similar patterns to those of traditional companies, although they measure their migration periods in quarters instead of years. They prove that growth moves in a spiral shape, no matter what corporate generation you belong to. The

Amazon.com spiral in Figure 7-2 looks almost exactly like those of Microsoft and Home Depot, with the period of heavy investment and infrastructure development coinciding with a temporary pullback in the share price. The difference, however, is that Microsoft and Home Depot migrated to simple growth, while Amazon.com slipped into underperformance. Yahoo! (see Figure 7-3) also followed a similar pattern, but sustained more of its growth momentum and is already migrating back toward value-building growth.

Gathering the rest of the headlines are companies that no one associates with the dot.com companies. They have the nuts-and-bolts parts in place, enjoy a deep, rich pool of human resources, have a portfolio of strong brands, but lack the drive and intensity to exploit them to the fullest. The valuations of most of these companies show that the market is enamored with the freshness and drive of the dot.coms, without really comprehending that both sets of companies lack the proper balance to survive in an e-business world. They have also not realized that each group needs exactly what the other has.

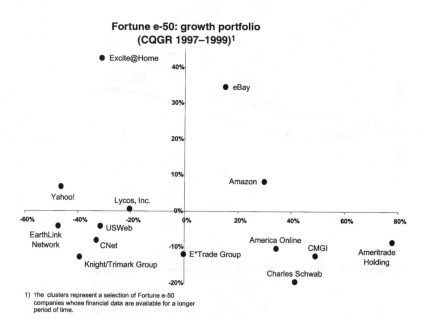

1) The clusters represent a selection of Fortune e-50 companies whose financial data are available for a longer period of time.

Figure 7-1 The Growth Matrix for leading e-companies.

Amazon.com

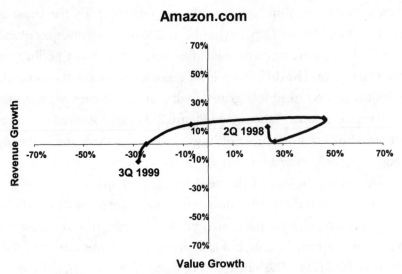

Figure 7-2   The migration of Amazon's center of gravity.

Yahoo!

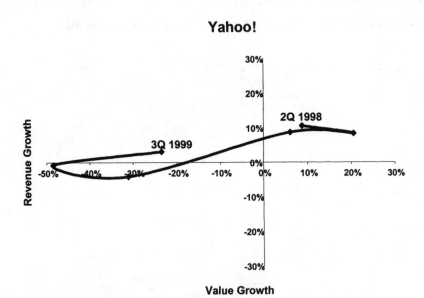

Figure 7-3   The migration of Yahoo!'s center of gravity.

If the e-companies and the more traditional companies are indeed complementary, it raises the question of who will win in the future? Our answer: Both can win, if they borrow from each other. Both types of companies have imbalances in their growth drivers, which means that their positions and their approaches—in their current forms— are not sustainable. The traditional companies lack growth determination and need improvements in certain other drivers. The dot.com companies have very powerful growth determination, but they often lack the support systems, the infrastructure, and the brand capital that comes only from years of proven success.

The winners in the future will combine the two and restore balance. Traditional companies need to learn from the dot.coms and rediscover the growth determination that made them success stories in the first place. Dot.com companies need to back up their vision, strategy, and strong corporate culture with the tools and business models that ensure and support ongoing growth. No company can build up and expand a value-building growth position without balance, which leads to the question: How do we bring these two halves together?

THE RULES MAY HAVE CHANGED . . .

Some companies know that achieving value-building growth in this environment means reestablishing the necessary balance to drive a company forward and generate superior shareholder value. Companies such as Nokia and Clear Channel Communications have succeeded in fusing a dot.com obsession with growth, consumer focus, innovation, and constant change with what are essentially early-twentieth-century businesses: telephones and broadcasting.

Other companies have made great strides from a position of deep underperformance and have almost returned to value-building growth. A current example is IBM. Investors may complain about Amazon.com's losses, but their red ink pales compared to the losses

143

IBM racked up in the early 1990s. That IBM rose from underperformance after losing almost $15 bn over three years represents a remarkable comeback fueled by a balance of the best that both dot.com companies and traditional companies have to offer. (See Figure 7-4.)

IBM, the company that once dominated the mainframe computer market and launched the mainstream personal computer experienced the culmination of the three worst years in the history of the company in 1992 to 1994. The losses erased a significant chunk of the money that the entire company had earned since it entered the PC market in 1982. By 1993 when CEO Lou Gerstner took over, IBM was buried deep among the underperformers.

But IBM is still around. By 1998, it had almost achieved value-building growth, after migrating through the profit seeker quadrant. In terms of the growth drivers, IBM has a solid basis for an enabling business model, and it has a strong resource and competency base, considerable network power through its many alliances and relationships, and strengths in structures and processes. Each of these areas was exploited and further optimized as IBM began to reshape and

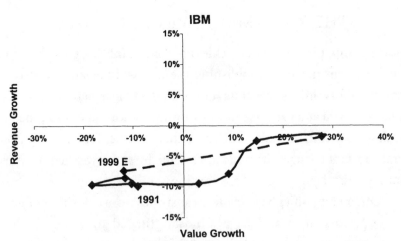

Figure 7-4 Leadership and legacy helped IBM recover from the depths of underperformance.

rebuild itself. In terms of its empathy with stakeholders, the company has a long history of investor relations and considerable brand equity.

What IBM lacked and regained—as soon as Lou Gerstner was on board—was growth determination in almost every aspect. The company needed a vision to guide its future growth, it needed firm leadership in order to change an entrenched organization, and it needed a better strategic understanding of its businesses and their prospects. It also needed to break with the rigid "silo" structure that inhibited development and change. It is interesting that IBM just recently changed its demonstrated growth determination to a more precise determination for accelerated growth.

This kind of organic turnaround is only one approach to restoring balance. The other approach is a merger, as exemplified by America Online and Time Warner in January 2000. In terms of balance, the merger makes considerable strategic sense because it brings together two distinct halves into a whole that is equipped to lead in the digital world. The union also has parallels to the cases discussed in Part 2. As Nokia demonstrated, in today's world sheer size combined with a product portfolio that is broad and deep is a powerful recipe for igniting rapid growth. This merger certainly fulfills that goal when you consider the media properties and the content the merger combines. Coupled with the subsequent purchase of EMI Music, the combined company now controls AOL, Netscape, CompuServe, CNN, the movie channel HBO, and an extensive cable television network on the media side, and the Warner Brothers and TNT cartoon and film libraries, the magazines *Time, Fortune,* and *Sports Illustrated,* and a music catalog that includes the Beatles and the Rolling Stones on the content side.

. . . BUT IT'S STILL BUSINESS

A company must focus on customer value and then shareholder value or its days are numbered. This means recognizing that engineering

LEARNING FROM THE PAST

Most companies on the stock market were hot stocks in their youth. Over the last 20 to 30 years, companies from the sixties and seventies that endured found the right balance across the growth drivers. Others suffered setbacks because they relied much too long on vision and an entrepreneurial culture alone. They could not create the proper balance:

- *Apple Computer.* The PC maker gained a loyal following with its personal computers and its Macintosh, launched in 1984. Apple fell to the ground because it did not find the right balance between technological innovation and customer interaction. The new and improved Apple, whose stock price rose sharply in 1999, succeeds precisely because it has begun to wed the wonders of virtual vision with the traditional ways of business. Steve Jobs, who has returned as CEO after a long absence from the company he cofounded in 1976, told *Fortune* magazine that Apple may have once been a bigger company, but it now has more talent and profitability than ever before.

- *Intel.* The chipmaker Intel, which went public in 1971, focused on building the infrastructure to sustain itself. This made Gordon Moore's vision of doubling chip capacity every 18 months a reality. In cyclical downturns, Intel would build greenfield computer plants that it could bring online as soon as demand turned up. It steadfastly refused to issue dividends, preferring instead to retain profits to fund its large-scale investment plans.

and design are means to end—namely, satisfying a customer—rather than ends in themselves. Not only the product but the entire customer experience must be appealing. AOL's history shows an adherence to this kind of philosophy, as the company—despite a storied history of technical setbacks and mishaps—consistently built its subscriber base by offering an easy-to-use way to enjoy the Internet. They made it easy to get online and keep coming back, which gave them a coolness that was almost antitech. The company's purchase of CompuServe in 1997 underscored this approach. AOL and the telecommunications company WorldCom (now MCI WorldCom) actually purchased together and divided the company up among themselves. AOL took the subscriber base and the content, while WorldCom inherited the plumbing infrastructure that ran the system.

Clear Channel's unique position boils down to a center of gravity, a mindset, that shows it knows its business and how to execute it. What is AOL Time Warner's business? It is exactly the same as Clear Channel's—it is a pure media company that exists to help advertisers reach their audiences and sell more products. An article in the *Economist* in late 1997 described AOL in those terms. In discussing AOL's shift to relying less on subscriber fees and more on advertising charges, the publication explained that at any given time, more people are "watching" AOL—by surfing or chatting—than are watching CNN or MTV. So why not advertise there? The Internet's tremendous growth naturally means that its "share of eyeballs" is rising with it, as people spend more time looking at their computer screens. These gains come by definition at the expense of other visual media such as print and television.

By merging, the two organizations gain the customer-driven approach, the size, breadth and depth of a Nokia, and the wealth of bundling opportunities exemplified by a Clear Channel, all in one move. There is no other organization right now that can reach as many people in as many different ways with recognized branded media products as AOL Time Warner. Nonetheless, some have argued that a high-flying Internet stock like AOL did not need to buy a Time Warner when it could have struck an alliance and cooperated with them. This argument overlooks one important fact: AOL needed to grow, and quickly. As Figure 7-5 shows, AOL had fallen from profit seeking to significant underperformance since mid-1998.

In stark contrast to Yahoo! and Amazon.com, which were either in a fall or recovering from one, AOL was clearly headed in the wrong direction. Since the beginning of 1998, there was no nine-month period in which the company achieved above-average growth, and the apparent stall began to take its toll on the company's share price, relative to other Internet stocks. Furthermore, much of AOL's subscriber base still depended on dial-up modems over slow, analog lines. When broadband technology took hold commercially, AOL stood to lose its customer base to faster connections if it had nothing comparable to offer.

Time Warner, meanwhile, had finally recorded gains after the long adjustment period following its merger with Warner in 1989. The company had made progress in breaking down fiefdoms and har-

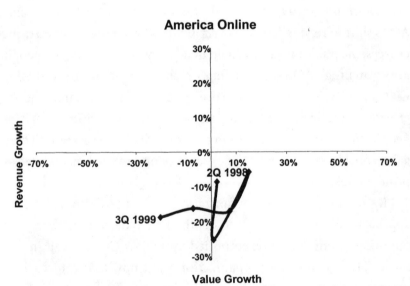

Figure 7-5 AOL's migration toward underperformance accelerated in late 1999.

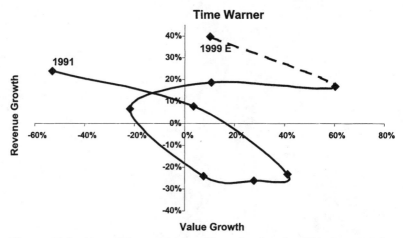

Figure 7-6 Time Warner had achieved value-building growth by 1997.

nessing its resources under a more holistic approach. Similar to FedEx, whose spiral Time Warner tracks almost exactly (see Figure 7-6), the company made the transformation from a simple grower into a value builder. By 1997 it had achieved value-building growth. But Time Warner was an outsider looking in as far as the Internet was concerned. It had the cable network that could be the vehicle for broadband Internet access, and it had the deep range of established media titles. But it lacked a way to jump-start itself as an Internet company, and it would risk losing its balance if it could not overcome this challenge.

The purchase of Time Warner by AOL not only created growth opportunities in the media, as described above. It also brought both companies out of positions that were not sustainable in their current form. It gave AOL a company that had achieved value-building growth after years of renewal and restructuring, and it gave Time Warner a proven entrée into the Internet.

The shape of tomorrow

SURVIVING AND THRIVING IN A POLARIZED WORLD

When the current clouds of e-dust finally settle, what fundamental effects will the "digital revolution" have had on the way companies grow? Discussions of technological convergence occasionally drown out a debate on that question, whose answers may have more far-reaching effects than any technical decision on a standard for a set-top box or a computer language.

Businesses urgently need to answer this question, as they plan for competition when the Internet becomes universal. As soon as most companies have embraced the Internet as a business enabler, the term *e-business*—and in fact, any term that has recently had the letter *e* fastened to its front—will lose its drawing power. Business will become business once again, although it will have been irrevocably transformed. But how deep will these changes be?

People have long expected technological advance to bring about fascinating social and economic changes, that "it" would finally happen. Many crystal balls showed that television would replace teachers, credit cards would replace cash, and personal computers would eliminate paper. All are still around in abundance. The "it" always happens, but it is rarely the "it" we expect.

Before different scenarios can be created to answer the question of how companies will grow in the future, one must first explore why the acceleration of technological progress is having any effect at all. The key involves knowing "why will business be different and how will these changes come about." In other words, what are the real underlying winds that will force every CEO to adjust and improve his or her navigation?

THE ICY WIND: INDUSTRIAL POLARIZATION

The Internet may well mark the greatest quantum leap in communications since Gutenberg introduced the Old World to movable type over 500 years ago. (The Chinese had invented movable type even earlier.) Marshall McLuhan argues in *Understanding Media* that the legacies of the printing press—in his words, the message of this medium—include the western world's appreciation and longing for mechanical and sequential thinking, for consistency and continuity. Countless things and processes, from assembly *lines* to supply *chains* to Lego building blocks, teach us that one thing leads to another and that all parts have their place. Even the term on*line* implies some kind of direct, linear connection over a cable.

McLuhan said in the early 1960s that what he called "automation"— the foreshadowing of today's digital situation—would end the Gutenberg legacy by creating discontinuities, upsetting order, and rendering sequences irrelevant. Under McLuhan's assumptions, if an object needs to move from point A to point B, the *only* thing that matters is that it arrives at point B. Everything that happened or could have happened between points A and B is irrelevant. We focus on the "1/0" outcome—that is, it arrived or it didn't. This is, of course, exactly how the Internet routes e-mail and conducts searches. The Internet was conceived over 30 years ago to be route independent and to ensure only that the package arrives at its destination, even in a full-scale nuclear war.

The end of comfort zones.   The use of binary—the 1's and 0's that underpin almost everything in contemporary life—have begun to alter our perceptions. We now think in terms of outcomes and are much less willing to accept excuses when these outcomes are not realized. We also think in terms of networks, or systems of 1's and 0's. In the business world, this results in mass customization, channel fragmentation, and supplier proliferation. Or in plain English, it means that businesses now have more markets to reach, and more ways to reach them more quickly than ever before. The same applies to their customers and suppliers, who can use these newfound options to navigate the network in order to bypass the parts they find unsatisfactory. For companies, this makes success mandatory. Being a little bit successful is like being a little bit pregnant.

In the future, everything will either be "on" or "off." Dell's customers have already switched computer retailers "off" by buying directly from the company. Record companies are being switched "off" by customers downloading their music directly. Customers turn eToys and Priceline.com "on" because they feel they find better prices or service. Companies such as Yahoo! and Excite can essentially measure their unit sales in hits—that is, the number of times customers have switched them on. In short, customers are increasingly able—and eager—to pull the goods and services they want from point *A* to point *B* in the most optimal way along the network.

Connectivity is displacing the old linear habits with a new networking mindset. Companies now need to think of themselves as nodes in a vast network rather than as links in a chain. Companies that exploit and broaden their connectivity in the network—that is, which generate hits—will not just survive, but thrive. Those that continue to build their business for a world where the only kinds of integration were vertical and horizontal will not last much longer. The polarization in the digital (binary) business world leaves no gray areas, no comfort zones, and no places for a business version of a Third Way. It represents another form of "grow up or fold up."

This notion is much more than a simple reflection of Silicon Valley *zeitgeist*. The two regions perceived as comfort zones in the

153

Growth Matrix are already disappearing, thus polarizing and disintegrating the matrix. Between 1995 and 1998, the population of simple growers and profit seekers—based on a sample of 4547 companies across industries and regions worldwide—dropped by 21 percent, swelling the ranks of the value builders and especially the underperformers. These two polar opposites accounted for a disproportionate 60 percent of all companies at the beginning of 1999.

The trend toward polarization—that is, the elimination of the comfort zones—was even sharper in certain industries considered to be major movers in e-business. The population of simple growers and profit seekers in the global automotive industry sank by 30 percent between 1995 and 1998, and plummeted by 55 percent in the telecommunications industry. In short, the growth matrices of the future will be dominated by value builders and underperformers. (See Figure 8-1.)

A continuation of this trend will concentrate the wealth in any given industry among a small minority of companies. These companies will have a solid center of gravity and will have achieved a proper

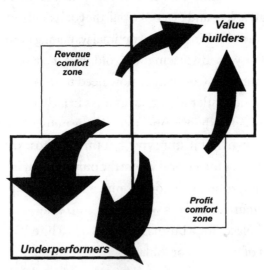

Figure 8-1 The Growth Matrix will undergo increasing polarization.

THE SHAPE OF TOMORROW

balance that will allow them to remain afloat and viable amid hyper-competition. The unbalanced simple growers and profit seekers will become rare, as most companies will underperform and eventually disappear.

This accelerated form of creative destruction will reallocate the resources of the underperformers, while eventually causing rifts among the hypercompetitors. We do not feel that the hypercompeti-tors who "win" the current weeding-out process will settle down into oligopolistic competition. Rather, we would argue that the dust will never settle. A constant state of vigilance is necessary, as this new breed of value builders needs to watch their front as well as their back.

The underperformers, meanwhile, should keep in mind that Joseph Schumpeter's phrase "creative destruction" means "destruction that creates" or even "destruction that liberates," and not "creative ways to destruct." Like the American passenger train stations that now serve as shopping and convention centers, much of the infrastructure of these companies will find other uses. Their human resources can apply their marketing, sales, management, and manufacturing exper-tise in the same industry or in emerging industries that could range from communications startups to commercial offshoots of the human genome project to the beginnings of space travel and colo-nization. One reader of *Fortune* magazine recently advised a college student that he should not worry that much about career planning. She now has a dream job that did not even exist 10 years ago. Who could have planned for that?

One industry that stands to capitalize on these displacements is training and education. Already one of the world's largest service indus-tries, education may sneak up on tourism as a major growth engine for many economies, as people slowly become accustomed to cradle-to-grave learning. Michael Milken, his brother Lowell, and Oracle CEO Larry Ellison have formed a company called Knowledge Universe that could serve as a model for other firms that want to provide corporate and private training programs as well as coaching programs.

Like entrepreneur Chris Whittle before them, they want to turn around the education market—which amounts to $650 bn in the United States alone—in the same way that private initiative took over healthcare over the last 15 to 20 years. Whittle pioneered in-classroom television with his Channel One project 10 years ago, and his Edison Company now manages public school systems on a for-profit basis.

The digital revolution: Even more polarization?   Some observers argue that the opportunities offered by connectivity and networked business will allow some of the less wealthy countries and regions to compete internationally and better exploit their comparative advantages. Software development in India and international call centers in Ireland are just two examples that encourage this view. One could also argue, however, that the sharp polarization emerging among value builders and underperformers will be accompanied by an even sharper polarization among regions and countries. Two facts clearly support the latter view:

- First, although the Internet has set records for its penetration rates, it is still used by a tiny fraction of the world's population, the majority of whom have never even made a telephone call, never mind logged into cyberspace. All the acceleration in the world won't bring enough people into the global network quickly enough to allow them to connect and interact. Furthermore, the "wealth gap"—the difference between average incomes in rich and poor countries—has also been rising geometrically. Taken at face value, these facts do not bode well for the utopian view that digital communications—of which the Internet is one manifestation—will be the great equalizer that spreads opportunities and wealth across the globe.

  One key element to reversing the wealth gap and preventing regional polarization is the continued refinement of affordable wireless communications technology. Tens of thousands of Chinese become new mobile telephone subscribers every day.

An entire generation will grow up without ever needing (or knowing how) to use telephones attached to cables.

- The second aspect to consider is *Metcalfe's law,* which says that the value of a network increases as a function of the number of participants. If the "network" as we have described it in this chapter is the template for new business models, it makes sense to grow the network. Adding participants to the network would take globalization beyond its current phase to a phase of interconnection, which lessens dependence and creates alternatives.

It is obviously impossible to know now whether the digital revolution will be the great equalizer or the great polarizer. Although the technology could make it happen, political differences and the legacy of trade barriers and traditions could still act as a brake on this progress.

THE WARM TRADE WIND: VALUE AS THE TRANSFORMER OF E-BUSINESS INTO V-BUSINESS

Value is the other underlying wind that will force every CEO to adjust and improve his or her navigation. It works in conjunction with the wind of polarization, and the two mutually reinforce each other. The reasons, once again, have to do with the proliferation of a networking mindset. This entrenches a feeling among customers that they are entitled to pull through what they want, when they want it, from wherever they can get it, with more or less full real-time knowledge of their alternatives.

This shift of power is dramatic, and its yardstick is value. Many traditional business models have been based on controlling what customers can get, when they can have it, and who can supply them, while relying on their customers' lack of information about alternatives. A degree of value was usually delivered, but the customers' perception of value was by definition incomplete or distorted. This meant that companies could make money for years or even decades by offering "good enough," without the need or expense of being the "very best." But the spread of information and the reduction of communication costs to virtually zero have rendered this model ineffective. These two trends have armed customers with an unprecedented amount of market transparency, a powerful poison to products and services that used to be good enough.

Generation Z children have a keener, clearer eye for value than their grandparents could have possibly had. Instead of being purely price oriented, they look for the optimal way to journey through the network to find what they want. Networks by nature mean more alternatives and more information, so Generation Z children can choose between the supplier who offers the lowest price or the coolest brand or the fastest delivery or simply the most fun while browsing around, . . . or any combination of the above. The effects on business-to-business transactions will be even stronger, as customers tap their connections and their broader pool of continually updated information to sort out less attractive alternatives and focus on the crispest, clearest value propositions. Many will do this in real-time auctions in which only vetted suppliers can participate.

The whole idea of the network is second nature in this world, which should come as no surprise. As soon as most offices and houses—and perhaps most street corners and shirt pockets—throughout the world have some access to the Internet, the whole concept of e-business will be taken for granted. After all, we have taken "t-business" for granted ever since the telephone became commonplace as a means for people to conduct business with other people a century earlier.

Deliver or self-destruct: There's no place to hide. The days of good enough are numbered. As the network increases in terms of users and nodes, competition will intensify for the creation of and control of the access points to the network. Competition will likewise intensify for the "content"—information, goods, or services—that flow through these access points. No matter how a company chooses, nurtures, and builds its connections, it faces a challenge with no middle ground: It needs to deliver or self-destruct. What really matters in the long run is not e-business but rather the creation and delivery of value, what one could call *v-business.*

One model for a v-business company involves a variety of content that could be delivered in a variety of channels. On the consumer side, AT&T and Citigroup have built their current strategies around this idea. AT&T has spent over $100 bn to acquire cable television operators, which in essence provide it additional access points to customers. Citigroup, meanwhile, has endeavored to break down old silo structures in financial services. The entire upside of the merger between Citibank and Traveler's Group rests on the combined group's ability to cross-sell. A person who contacts Citibank theoretically has an access point to insurance, brokerage services, and credit cards as well as personal banking, all of which are now under the Citigroup umbrella.

Simply being in the network—or, in this case, welcoming someone into a network—will have limited value, as customers and competitors become increasingly adept at switching undesirable or uninteresting roadblocks to off. Many bricks-and-mortar retailers will experience frustration as their new portals fail to draw hits, as Wal-Mart's originally did. Such Web sites will remain off until customers have a compelling reason to go there.

The current battle among booksellers offers insights into differences in e-business, which is really v-business in disguise. The much publicized competition in the United States among Barnes and Noble, Books-A-Million, Borders, and Amazon.com has little to do with books, and a lot to do with benefits. The online sellers offer efficiency, ease of use, selection, and price. The bricks-and-mortar businesses sell experience and escape. They surround the customer with coffee shops, comfortable reading areas, promotional events, and other like-minded people. As each group enhances and communicates these differentiating factors, the question of "which side will win?" becomes irrelevant. Each side will win its share, as long as customers continue to attach value to the benefits offered.

The same has long applied to recorded music. People do not go to a club or attend a live concert solely to hear a particular song. They can do that at home or in their car whenever they choose. They go to clubs and live concerts for the experience, or for social reasons. Clubs and concerts provide added benefits that a compact disc cannot provide on its own. To talk of one putting the other out of business is absurd.

No Way Around Value-Building Growth. A successful v-business company, then, is ultimately synonymous with a value grower, one whose fundamental principles will still obtain in the distant future. The strategic balance between revenue growth and economic earnings will remain essential. Revenue growth is the lifeblood of a networked world, which depends on relationships, information, interaction, and active alternatives. Uncontrolled expansion or a narrow focus on efficiency and profit will lead investors and customers to switch a company to off more quickly than ever before, choking off the comfort zones of simple growth and profit seeking.

The relationship between company environment and growth drivers will remain broadly the same as well. Despite rapid and destabilizing shifts across external factors, growth will remain a self-driven pursuit. Likewise, companies will still need to strike a balance among growth determination, empathy with stakeholders, and business enablers. Their growth determination will still involve the definition of a clear vision, combined with a strategy and a strong leadership team to execute it. Empathy with stakeholders will still require that a company be continually aligned with the shifting interests of employees, customers, suppliers, and investors. Business enablers such as information technology, research and development, and alliances will allow the company to build new connections in the network while keeping existing ones free of bottlenecks and barriers.

Appendix 1

A.T. KEARNEY'S VALUE-BUILDING GROWTH STUDY

A.T. Kearney's Growth Database comprises a comprehensive set of data and financial information on over 20,000 companies and covers more than 98 percent of the world's market capitalization with 8000 American, 6400 European, and 5600 Asian/Pacific companies.

The data were gathered from commercial databases, especially from *WorldScope*™. Accuracy of all data has been cross-checked with other commercial databases, for example, *CompuStat*™, *Moody's*, *Amadeus*, and annual company reports. A new database covering financial analyses and growth ratios was developed based on all data collected.

A.T. Kearney's study is aligned to the accounting principles as detailed in the *WorldScope*™ *Handbook*. Our analysis covered a 12-year period from 1988 to 1999. The database was last updated in spring 2000.

In many cases, analyses had to be entered manually by using a subset of 1100 companies. Key criteria for selecting the companies were market capitalization and revenue.

DEFINING INDUSTRIES AND PEER GROUPS

For benchmarking purposes, a major and minor industry SIC code was assigned to each company to indicate its specific industry. Theoretically,

Region	Target countries	Countries excluded due to low market capitalization	Filter market capitalization	Total number of remaining companies
America	• Canada • Mexico • United States	–	• > US$ 5 bn	317

Asia	• Japan (122)
	• Korea (50)
	• Australia (68)
	• Rest of Asia (139)
	  – China
	  – Hong Kong
	  – India
	  – Indonesia
	  – Malaysia
	  – The Philippines
	  – Singapore
	  – Taiwan
	  – Thailand
		• China and the Philippines	• > US$ 2.5 bn	335

Europe	• Austria • Belgium • Denmark • Finland • France • Germany • Greece • Ireland • Italy • Luxembourg • The Netherlands • Norway • Portugal • Spain • Sweden • Switzerland • Turkey • United Kingdom	–	• > US$ 3 bn	347

companies with comparable minor industry SIC codes are considered direct peers, whereas companies with comparable major industry SIC codes operate in the same industry and thus within the realm of comparable success factors.

In exceptional cases, a company's competitive position cannot be adequately determined by automatically assigning codes and grouping companies. For this valuation, the peer group was adjusted manually based on publicly available data and industry experts' opinions.

A category of nonspecific industries was set up to benchmark companies not allocated to a particular industry.

Region	Target countries	Filter sales	Total number of remaining companies
America	• Canada • Mexico • United States	• > US$ 10 bn	133
Asia	• Japan (122) • Korea (50) • Australia (68) • Rest of Asia (139) – Hong Kong – India – Indonesia – Malaysia – Singapore – Taiwan – Thailand	• > US$ 8 bn	129
Europe	• Austria • Belgium • Denmark • Finland • France • Germany • Greece • Ireland • Italy • Luxembourg • The Netherlands • Norway • Portugal • Spain • Sweden • Switzerland • Turkey • United Kingdom	• > US$ 12 bn	128

TIME FRAMES, GEOGRAPHY, AND AVERAGES

Three sets of time frames were used in this study: a maximum 12-year time frame; a medium 5-year time frame ("a CEO's typical life span"), and a year-to-year time frame.

Encompassing companies across all major industrial and economic centers around the world, this is a truly global study.

As a yardstick, a company's peer group was its global industry. For the few cases in which global competitors could not be identified, regional peer groups were chosen instead. Weighted averages per peer group were calculated, indicating the time frame, region, and peer

Region	Companies added because of high sales despite low or no MC
America	• Costco Companies Inc. not included in MC ranking
Asia	• Nippon Life Insurance Company • Dai-Schi Mutual Life Insurance • Tomen Corp. • Sumitomo Life Insurance • Nichimen Corp. • Meij Life Insurance Company • Kanematsu Corp. • Asaki Mutural Life Insurance Company • Peregine Investment Holding Ltd. • Toyota Tsusho Corp. • Norinchukin Bank • Kawasaki Corp. • Seiyu Ltd.
Europe	• Quelle Schickedanz • Electricité de France • France Télécom • Robert Bosch GmbH • Enel • Deutsche Bahn AG • WestLB • Adam Opel AG • SHV Holdings N.V. • Den Norske Stats Objeskap

group. When calculating averages, filters were used to prevent data distortion from extreme outliers (-100 percent $<$ compounded annual growth rate < 150 percent).

MEASURING GROWTH

"Value-building growth" is based on two main indicators of growth:

- Revenue growth to measure the quantity of growth
- Adjusted market capitalization (value growth) for measuring the quality of growth

This pragmatic framework does not discredit other potential growth indicators. At the beginning of the project, numerous quantitative and qualitative growth indicators were discussed and tested. Characteristics of the indicators we used are the following:

- Broad acceptance among our clients, our consultants, and third-party experts

- Strictly positive numbers other than zero to calculate CAGR

- Availability from commercial databases across countries and industries

Revenue Growth

- Revenue growth measures sales for one company within one year.

- Nominal values are used.

- The definition of *revenue* may differ across specific industries. For banks (see chart), revenue represents a company's total operating revenue, as follows:

  - Interest and fees on loans

  - Interest on federal funds

  - Interest on bank deposits

  - Interest on state, county, and municipality funds

  - Interest on U.S. government and federal agencies' securities

  - Federal funds sold and securities purchased under resale agreements

  - Lease financing

  - Net leasing revenue

  - Income from trading accounts

  - Foreign exchange income

Ratio	Abbreviation	Equation
Growth rate	• CAGR	• $[(\text{End/beginning})^{1/n-1}] - 1$ • n: period in years
Equity	• E	• Total assets minus total liabilities
Adjusted market capitalization	• AMC	• Market capitalization minus $\text{equity}_{(n)}$ plus $\text{equity}_{(n-1)}$ • n: this year; n: 1 minus previous year

- Profit and losses from investment securities
- Service charges on deposits
- Other service fees
- Trust income
- Commissions and fees
- For insurance companies, revenue is represented by the following:
  - Premiums earned
  - Investment income (If a company reports this item net of expenses, then the net amount is shown after deduction of interest expense.)
  - Other operating income
  - Profit and/or losses from securities sales (pretax)
- Revenue criteria for other financial companies are as follows:
  - Investment income
  - Interest income
  - Income from trading accounts
  - Trust income
  - Commissions and fees
  - Rental income
  - Securities purchased under resale agreements
  - Investment banking income
  - Principal transactions

Adjusted Market Capitalization (AMC) Growth

- AMC growth is calculated based on market capitalization that is adjusted by changes in equity. Market capitalization is calculated by the total number of shares and the year-end stock price.
- Nominal values are used

- There are two advantages of calculating CAGR only for market capitalization:
  - Issuance of new shares leads to adjustments
  - Divestments or spinoffs lead to adjustments
- Adjusted equity can be managed with less complexity than total shareholder return (TSR).
- Additionally, analyses clearly underscore the strong correlation between AMC and other key value ratios, for example, TSR.

ASSUMPTIONS

Assuming comparative purchasing power parity, all data have been converted into U. S. dollars based on year-end exchange rates. Detailed tests revealed the following:

- Over the long term, all relevant currencies remained relatively stable with less than 1 percent impact on corporate CAGR revenue.

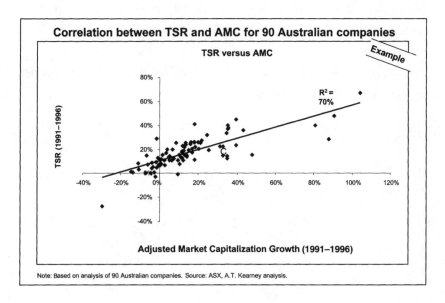

Note: Based on analysis of 90 Australian companies. Source: ASX, A.T. Kearney analysis.

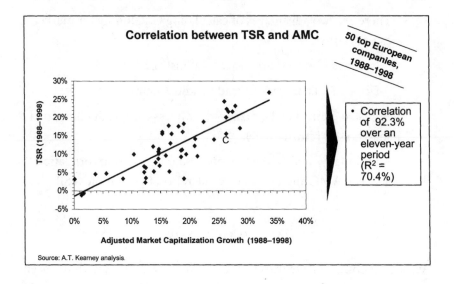

Source: A.T. Kearney analysis.

- In the short term, fluctuations had a higher impact, but this was limited to parts of the database (certain European countries and Asia) and was compensated by high sales internationally.

Evaluations of stock markets do not include premiums or discounts. Major stock market trends were eliminated by benchmarking companies against peers. No regional trends were identified other than those based on general assumptions.

A.T. Kearney's Value-Building Growth Study did not focus on risk aspects, for example, beta tests.

Appendix 2

CEOS' ANSWERS TO GROWTH-RELATED QUESTIONS

Answers given by more than 300 CEOs and other top managers during A.T. Kearney executive briefings and meetings cast a light on the degree to which corporate leaders worldwide understand the true mechanisms of growth.

The questions were phrased in such a way that straight answers resulted:

- *Why should a company grow?* While 68 percent answered "to generate superior value," the remaining 32 percent voted for "to obtain a superior strategic position."

- *To what extent does your company exploit its growth potential?* Executives rated their own degree of fulfillment 4.5 on a scale from 1 (low) to 8 (high).

- *What are the main barriers to growth?*
  - Organization and leadership (42 percent)
  - Cultural resistance (17 percent)
  - Operational competence gaps (17 percent)
  - Unattractive regulatory environment (17 percent)

- Economic downturn (7 percent)
- *What is the main driver for shareholder value?*
  - Sustainable growth (37 percent)
  - Economic value added (28 percent)
  - Profitability (19 percent)
  - Charismatic CEO (9 percent)
  - Exciting new products (7 percent)
- *Which are the main routes to value-building growth?*
  - Market share increase (50 percent)
  - White space opportunities (29 percent)
  - Geographical expansion (15 percent)
  - Diversification (6 percent)
- *Which is the superior way of value-building growth?*
  - Internal, through stretch of resources (60 percent)
  - External, through acquisitions (40 percent)
- *What next steps to growth are you planning?*
  - Develop the company's growth cycle position and derive the main strategic reorientation. (50 percent)
  - Identify cultural growth stoppers. (21 percent)
  - Think about the right path to grow. (13 percent)
  - Discover internal growth barriers. (9 percent)
  - Collect more information about the competition. (7 percent)

Appendix 3

A.T. KEARNEY'S FOUR-STEP VALUE GROWTH APPROACH

Growth of a company can be achieved by trial and error. Growth can also be achieved by favorable external conditions and good luck. But first and foremost—as the case studies in this book indicate—growth can be achieved by taking a systematic approach.

Over the years, A.T. Kearney has developed a four-step value growth approach that not only demonstrates that growth can be learned but also explains how to do it (see Figure A3-1). The deliverables of a project executed using this approach are an assessment of the growth position the company finds itself in at the outset of any growth initiative as well as an assessment of the value growth potential that they could realize in their position and in their environment. On this basis, a focused growth concept and tangible growth initiatives can be developed.

The approach to be put in action to achieve these results has a generic starting point but can be adjusted to each growth quadrant's needs: While simple growers need to reorient toward value, which means achieving balance between growing and saving, underperformers at the same time have to do much more. Drastic restructuring of the entire company is unavoidable, including the value orientation

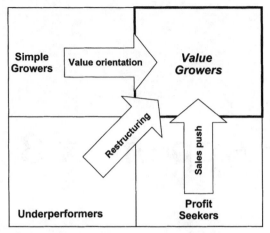

Figure A3-1 Basic growth strategies.

that the simple growers have to perform as well. On the other hand, their restructuring has to include higher sales in order to edge up to the value grower position. At the same time, the profit seekers have to let go of their cost consciousness and adopt a more customer-oriented selling approach.

Whatever the basic growth lever is, companies that follow the four-step value growth approach will find themselves in a growth mode sooner than those who have declared growth to be an externally induced development.

Before starting this kind of project, it is essential to make sure that the whole company is committed to the growth initiative.

STEP 1: ESTABLISH THE VALUE GROWTH POSITION

Without a clear assessment of a company's or a business unit's present and past position in the Growth Matrix, it will be hard to decide which way is the right way to make value-building growth a reality. Before doing anything, the position has to be crystal clear. That is why the first activity has to be assessing and benchmarking the growth position (see Figure A3-2):

- For this purpose a growth database has to be developed, peer companies have to be identified, and their historical data as well as the company's own data have to be entered into a database that allows for time series analyses of companies and scatter diagrams mirroring whole industries that put the respective growth position into perspective.

- To create internal benchmarks, the financial position down to business unit level has to be evaluated. This analysis can be based on the company's own data complemented by data acquired from neutral external sources. In this context value ratios can be adjusted and standardized—for example, substitute AMC with EBIT or other indicators, if necessary.

- Moreover, all financial data plus competitor and industry data have to be carefully analyzed in order to create external bench-

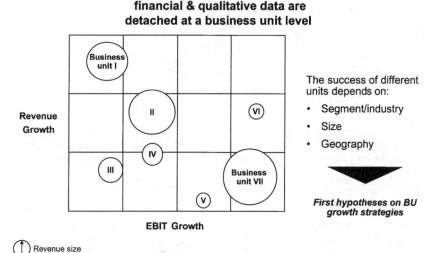

Figure A3-2 Growth positions of business units in comparison.

marks, lessons learned, and initial hypotheses about where and what the value levers are.

- Based on the internal and external data, a customized growth diagnostic is developed that follows the growth drivers and enables a clear understanding of the current growth situation of the entire company, the business unit, or even product lines.

- Before the diagnostics are actually put into action, any existing growth initiatives have to be audited and challenged. The means and modes of growth have to be obtained and understood from the data. Gaps between targeted and actual results of these growth initiatives have to be identified. This enables the team to understand a company's growth profile and potential growth alternatives.

A map of growth initiatives makes it easy to compare the quantified impact of growth moves with the growth targets set by the company. For example, the gap between current target and actual performance can be expressed in terms of revenue and time (Figure A3-3).

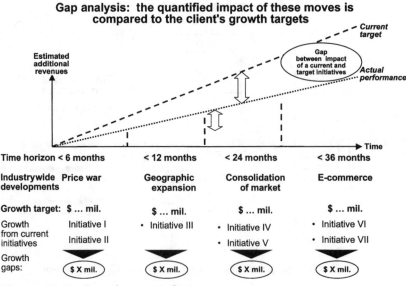

Figure A3-3 Growth gap analysis.

Looking at the phase "geographic expansion," there is a time as well as a revenue gap: After 12 months the geographic expansion has not reached the targeted scope or, looking at it from a different angle, 12 months was not enough to fully reach the target. The growth gap in general is best expressed as revenue gap in millions of dollars, which is the best indicator of what has been left out.

Once an initial idea of the company's current growth position becomes clear, the team can move on to the next step, which is even more demanding. It is about performing the actual growth diagnostic, which means exploring data with the aim of understanding much more about one's own company and the industry.

STEP 2: PERFORM THE GROWTH DIAGNOSTIC

It is crucial to not perform the growth diagnostic in a superficial, generic way. Rather, the general diagnostic concept has to become an individual tool customized to a company's specific needs. First, it has to be understood and second, fine-tuned based on the basic self-assessment done in step 1. Based on that, interactive diagnostics are performed across the whole supply chain—"suppliers, company, customers"—and for direct competition. Additionally, growth gaps identified in the first step are analyzed in detail and growth opportunities are collected and screened.

- To explore growth opportunities and prepare for tailoring the respective activities, workshops have to be conducted. During these workshops, the growth teams learn to identify with the common goal. Workshops should take place at a minimum of two breakpoints during the growth project:
  - One growth workshop should be conducted at the beginning of the diagnostic phase in order to help people understand the concept and narrow the focus down to the most important growth drivers.

- The second and even more important workshop with the whole team becomes necessary toward the end of step 2 as this is when the findings so far are summarized, existing growth opportunities are discussed, and additional initiatives are identified.
- Besides workshops, the second step of the growth diagnostic is an in-depth self-assessment that goes beyond the assessment of the growth position as executed in step 1. This self-assessment is based on a questionnaire exploring a company's internal growth perception. It is built around a growth vision, the ambitiousness of growth targets, the company's market approach (lines of business and so on), and the individual growth barriers as seen by the person or the team that performs the assessment. Another issue to be covered is the incentives people expect from actively supporting growth initiatives.
- Once the self-assessment has clarified most of the key issues, it is time to find out more about the company's whole supply chain. Diagnostic interviews explore the external topography as well as the internal growth "arsenal":
  - While "external" includes all macro impacts, technical discontinuities, and the competitive configuration as well as influences related to the ownership structure,
  - The internal drivers are much more important than the external ones. Internally the growth arsenal encompasses the growth determination in the company as well as empathy with stakeholders, which means closeness to and deep understanding of all issues that customers as well as suppliers, shareholders, employees, and, of course, the community consider important. A business model then needs to be developed to enable intrinsic growth.
- Based on that understanding, the growth team has to dig one level deeper to find the actual growth drivers. It is one of the findings of the study this book is based on that the internal

growth arsenal is often more telling than the external drivers. Knowing the internal drivers well means holding the key to untapped growth potential.

- Based on the answers to the growth diagnostics questionnaire and the self-assessment, a detailed benchmarking can be carried out. For this purpose each growth driver is compared to carefully selected best practices and the single best company (see Figure A3-4).

- Potential growth initiatives are derived from the gaps or strengths identified in the benchmarking—for example, functional bottlenecks, cultural barriers or, on the positive side, a market-oriented organization and a strong corporate culture.

These initiatives are carried out for each driver. If there is a gap in the growth vision but overall positive cost consciousness, the company has to go for value that would mean establishing investor intimacy and buy-in from stakeholders while not giving up cost consciousness (see Figure A3-5).

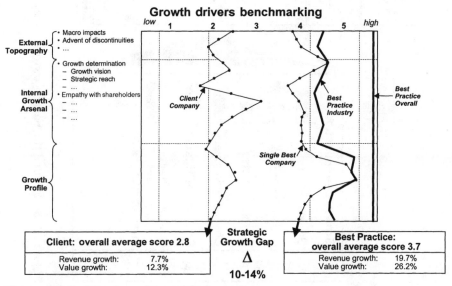

Figure A3-4 Benchmarking of first results.

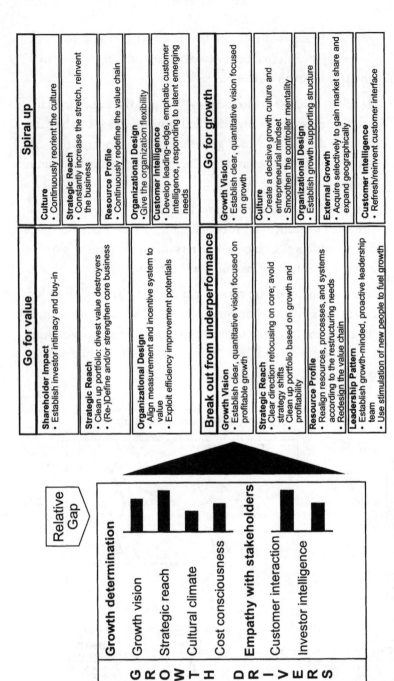

Figure A3-5 Finding the basic growth strategy.

The impact of each insufficient growth driver on the required tactical and strategic moves is then estimated, and targets are set accordingly.

Until now, the growth team has been working very theoretically and has done a lot of desk research and paperwork. In the third step the picture will change completely. It will be operational practice instead of vision and strategy.

STEP 3: DESIGN THE GROWTH WAVE

While designing how to tackle the growth topic in day-to-day operations, the team will work with all others much more closely than in the first two steps. Therefore, designing will not only mean blueprinting something that will become reality in the distant future. Instead, there will be a more or less parallel development in the planning and piloting of initiatives that seem appropriate but still have to pass the reality check:

- What is most important at the beginning of the practical part is a growth spearhead. The growth team that has been working so far therefore has to be reshuffled in order to now meet the needs of the targeted growth opportunities. What is now needed is more than just researchers and thinkers. The company on the brink of a growth initiative needs a set of spearheads who assume responsibilities for the action-oriented part of the project including communication. These people have to be flexible, open, hands-on experts for the different relevant fields. Their role unfolds as the action plan for the different growth initiatives is detailed and operationalized:

  - Just like any planning, this step starts with a time schedule and the allocation of responsibilities.

  - Part of the detailing work is in the field of strategy. This is where the experts come in. Strategic options have to be developed from the drivers, which will be the most important part of the strategic blueprint (see Figure A3-6).

- Taking that blueprint one step further is the roadmap to implement tactical and strategic moves.

- Based on this roadmap, growth moves are detailed toward a balanced approach:

  - They can be part of the very basic "bursting of functional bottlenecks," which has to be the first activity in a company that has stopped growing altogether. This company would push for a breakthrough in product and service quality, would increase sales with new customers through new channels, and would, on the other hand, improve supplier relationships, consider outsourcing, and so on.

  - Once a company unlocks its chain of "old ways," it has to move ahead and break down or eliminate the structural and process barriers that are leftover symptoms of the illness already cured. Processes have to be redesigned for the new approach to the supply market as well as to customers. Organizational structures and competencies then have to be adjusted for growth. To motivate the entire staff to support all activities, the company has to adjust its evaluation system and design a new remuneration system.

  - From this position it will be much easier for the company to leverage core capabilities in order to achieve substantial growth. If the company's market approach is no longer quite clear, this is the perfect time to phase out activities that no longer fit the portfolio or to acquire companies with competencies complementary or parallel to those of the core business.

    This can improve a company's value proposition tremendously, and it might even open up doors to gain a footing in new regional markets or in new related market segments or to supply "old" markets via entirely new channels.

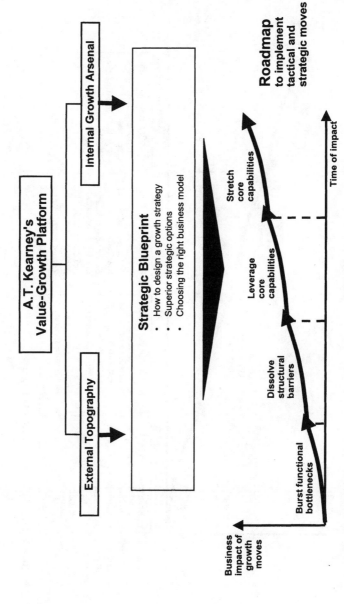

Figure A3-6 Value growth: From blueprint to roadmap.

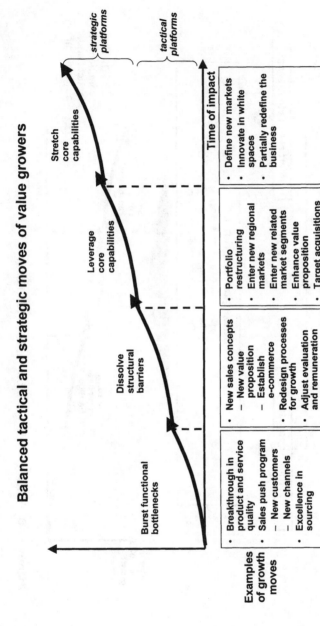

Figure A3-7 Growth moves over time.

- Once this position is safeguarded and already showing the first signs of success, it is time to stretch core capabilities. The company has to define new products and new markets while at the same time staying focused. It should work on developing ideas on how to exploit white space opportunities. It should also be flexible enough to partially redefine the business in line with changing customer demand (see Figure A3-7).

STEP 4: RIDE THE GROWTH WAVE

Once a company has started to design the future growth wave, it has also started to grow. In the fourth step it is therefore paramount to sustain the momentum that has been created along the initial steps. Growth is not growth that stops after one or two spectacular initiatives are completed. Growth has to be worked on in a well-balanced way. And if the growth topography or the internal growth arsenal change in any respect, the growth plan has to be adjusted in an iterative way. There is no final growth plan.

Index